The First Port of Call for Students of Evangelism

> — Leonard Sweet,
> Author, *SoulTsunami*

The emerging culture presents the Church with new challenges and opportunities for nearly every aspect of the proclamation and ministry of the Gospel. In *More Ready Than You Realize* Brian McLaren offers fresh perspectives on the practice of evangelism in the postmodern setting, proposing a metaphorical shift from "evangelism as argument" to "evangelism as conversation" in a clear, informed, and engaging way.

> — John R. Franke, D. Phil.,
> Associate Professor of Theology,
> Biblical Theological Seminary

My only question after reading Brian's new book is: Does Alice have any other writings published?

But seriously, Brian has helped rescue us from pushy sales techniques, 17 verses of "Just as I am" while we wait for those in the balcony, and of course big hair.

This book makes me want to reach for the volume knob…

> — Rob Bell,
> Teaching Pastor,
> Mars Hill Bible Church

Let me read anything Brian McLaren writes, and I'll be thinking in new ways immediately. Brian speaks with more practical clarity than any author I know who's engaging the postmodern discussion. And just as he did with *A New Kind of Christian*, the dialogical approach in *More Ready Than You Realize* will pull you along and put meat on the bones of this critical discussion.

> — Mark Oestreicher,
> Publisher, Youth Specialties and
> Emergent YS resources
> for emerging church leaders

Books by Brian McLaren

A Is for Abductive (with Leonard Sweet and Jerry Haselmayer)
The Church on the Other Side
Finding Faith
More Ready Than You Realize

More Ready Than You Realize

EVANGELISM AS DANCE
IN THE POSTMODERN
MATRIX

BRIAN D. MCLAREN

GRAND RAPIDS, MICHIGAN 49530

We want to hear from you. Please send your comments about this book to us in care of the address below. Thank you.

GRAND RAPIDS, MICHIGAN 49530

w w w . z o n d e r v a n . c o m

ZONDERVAN™

More Ready Than You Realize
Copyright © 2002 by Brian D. McLaren

Requests for information should be addressed to:

Zondervan, *Grand Rapids, Michigan 49530*

Library of Congress Cataloging-in-Publication Data

McLaren, Brian D., 1956–
    More ready than you realize : evangelism as dance in the postmodern matrix /
Brian D. McLaren.
      p. cm.
    Includes bibliographical references.
    ISBN 0-310-23964-8
    1. Evangelistic work—Case studies. 2. Postmodernism—Religious
aspects—Christianity—Case studies. I. Title.
BV3793 .M355 2001
269'.2–dc21   2001045663

Interior design by Nancy Wilson

Printed in the United States of America

---

03 04 05 06 07 08 09 /❖ DC/ 10 9 8 7

This book is dedicated to my parents, Dr. Ian and Virginia (Ginnie) McLaren. They have lived the gospel in beautiful and sacrificial ways. They have always opened their home and welcomed to their table friends and strangers alike. When their sons would bring home friends by the ones or twos or dozens, my parents always accepted those friends with warmth and love and without judgment—including those friends who, back in the 70s, were culturally so different from my parents . . . typically long-haired and barefooted, wildly (or barely) dressed, and sometimes in need of a good bath! That hospitality is an essential element of the disciple-making process this book explores, and it makes the gospel of Jesus Christ visible and tangible and flavorful and unforgettable. Most of what I know about being a Christian they showed me, without words, by the "conversation" of their lives. Thank you, Mom and Dad.

Contents

Acknowledgments

First and foremost I must, of course, acknowledge Alice, the real-life person whose privacy I have sought to protect here with a pseudonym. The pseudonym may be needless, however, because "Alice" will probably be heard with a voice (and real name) of her own in the years ahead, and will make ongoing contributions to the cause this book seeks to advance.

As well, I wish to acknowledge the staff, Leadership Team, members, and friends of Cedar Ridge Community Church, who have created a place where people can belong before they believe ... a faith community dedicated to helping people be and make disciples of Jesus Christ, in authentic community, for the good of the world. Thanks for so graciously sharing my time and attention with others, and affording me time to write and share what we are learning together. Any good that comes from my efforts in writing and speaking is really *our* accomplishment. I am so grateful for our partnership in the gospel.

Introduction

I don't know anything about dancing, really. My wife will tell you (and my kids will *really* tell you) that I'm no Fred Astaire, John Travolta, Michael Jackson, or Arthur Murray. I've got the "moves" of Mr. Rogers or Barney the Dinosaur. I dance like I golf—very seldom and more for my partner's entertainment and comic relief than anything else.

As a boy in elementary school, I remember my teachers trying to teach square dancing to our classes. We prepubescent boys wouldn't be caught dead touching girls, even though the girls (more mature by far) seemed interested in our cooperation. So, we would make a big show of spitting on our hands so the girls would not want to touch us. Needless to say, whatever I was supposed to learn about dance back then, I didn't.

I came from a religious home that did not allow dancing. True, as a teenager I sneaked in a few slow dances at parties here and there, but I never really got the hang of popular dancing. When I met my wife, my rhythmic deficiencies were to her something between a sad disappointment and a severe embarrassment. I shared her assessment.

When I was a teacher, I had a wonderful stint teaching English as a second language to the Cambodian Classical Ballet who arrived in the U.S. as refugees during the 1980s. My wife and I hosted several parties for our students, and inevitably a "boom box" would appear with cassette tapes of Khmer music. Soon the students would be in a circle, moving to the gentle Asian rhythm of the songs, knees bent and toes pointed, wrists and fingers forming graceful arcs at angles oblique to Western coordination. And of course they had to get the teacher to join in. I must have looked like a slow motion movie of a person who was being stung by a swarm of bees. Anyway, I am no dancer, by Eastern or Western standards.

Of course, I appreciate dance. I love to watch others dance. From time to time, we have liturgical dance in the worship services at Cedar Ridge Community Church, where I serve as pastor. I am nearly always in tears as I watch the beauty of dance performed to the glory of God.

I do know, however, just enough about dance to know that it provides a metaphor for something I care about a great deal. The theological term for this great love of mine is *evangelism*, but that word is so bastardized that I can hardly bear to use it. It is a word with a good heart, in spite of its dirty reputation. Allow me to prove this to you.

On the street, evangelism is equated with pressure. It means selling God as if God were vinyl siding, replacement windows, or a mortgage refinancing service. It means shoving your ideas down someone's throat, threatening him with hell if he does not capitulate to your logic or Scripture-quoting. It means excluding everyone from God's grace except those who agree with the evangelizer (a.k.a. evangelist). When preceded by the word *television*, the word *evangelism* grows even darker, more sinister—sleazy even. It means rehearsed, mechanical monologues, sales pitches, spiels, unrequested sermons or lectures, crocodile tears, uncomfortable confrontations sometimes made worse by Nutrasweet smiles and over-done eye contact and too-sincere professions of love for one's soul and concern for one's eternal destiny. ("Yeah, right. The truth is, you're trying to get more human fuel for your religious machinery—another convert, another notch in the belt, another victory for your ideology.")

This is the reputation evangelism has for most people. But consider this:

What if there really is a great and good and kind God, and we humans really are God's creatures, though we lose our way sometimes? And what if our deepest dream is really true, that the God who really exists really loves us? And what if one of the best ways for God to get through to those of us who have lost our way is via the kindness and influence of those others who have been brought back to a good path? And what if for every obvious and sleazy religious huckster there are in fact a dozen subtle but sincere examples of spiritual authenticity and vibrancy whose influences would do the rest of us a lot of good? What if there really are "angels" out there—not of the wings-and-halos type, but of the flesh-and-blood, laughter-and-tears type—people who are literally sent by God to intervene, to help those of us who have mucked up our lives, to give us a taste of grace, a "rumor of glory," as songwriter Bruce Cockburn says?

And what if you and I, who begin as wandering and confused people, could be so helped by our caring God-sent and love-filled friends that we could join them as messengers of grace, carriers of good news, secret-agent angels, case studies in God's power to change, enrich, fill, and rescue lives that were being wasted, ruined, self-sabotaged?

Consider for a moment if it is not evangelism, but rather late-twentieth-century styles of evangelism that deserve our disdain and avoidance. What if evangelism is one of the things that our world needs most?

After all, most people want to talk about things that really matter—their sense of God, their experiences of meaning or transcendence, their attempts to cope with their own mortality, their struggles with guilt and goodness, their dreams and hopes and deepest longings. They want to talk about these things because without them, all that is left in life is reruns and shopping, copulation and digestion, earning and spending and saving, culminating in estate sales and probate.

True, evangelism as it is commonly practiced and understood is debased. But what's left if we can't find a way for people to connect and explore together matters of ultimate concern? What's left if we can't find spiritually open friends with whom to converse about our deepest dreams and longings? Getting buttonholed in the street by a so-called evangelist is rough, but living life with nothing but a channel-changer and small talk about sports, work, office politics, and weather ain't so hot either.

Let me offer this better vision of good evangelism and good evangelists: Good evangelists—the kind we will talk about in this book—are people who engage others in good conversation about important and profound topics such as faith, values, hope, meaning, purpose, goodness, beauty, truth, life after death, life before death, and God. They do this, not because they like to be experts and impose their views on others, but because they feel they are in fact sent by God to do so. They live with a sense of mission that their God-given calling in life is not just to live selfishly, or even just to live well, but to in fact live unselfishly and well *and* to help others live unselfishly and well too. Evangelists are people with a mission from God and a passion to love and serve their neighbors. They want to change the world. They are mutants in the planet's spiritual evolution, if you will—good mutants whose new genes are desperately needed by the gene pool at large.

Good evangelism is the process of being friendly without discrimination and influencing all of one's friends toward better living, through good deeds and good conversations. For a Christian like myself, evangelism means engaging in these conversations in the spirit and example of Jesus Christ. (If you are not a committed Christian yourself, I am sure you will understand that since Christian commitment is where I'm coming from, it is the approach of this book. This is not to say there isn't a place for Buddhist or Hindu or Jewish evangelism, but someone else will be better suited to write on those topics.)

If you know anything about Jesus at all, you probably know that he was an amazing conversationalist. Unlike the typical evangelist-caricature of the late twentieth and early twenty-first centuries, Jesus was short on sermons, long on conversations; short on answers, long on questions; short on abstractions and propositions, long on stories and parables; short on telling you what to think, long on challenging you to think for yourself; short on condemning the irreligious, long on confronting the religious. (See Appendix A for a list of some of Jesus' conversations along with some discussion questions, so you and your friends can converse about Jesus' conversations.)

This is the kind of evangelism we are going to explore in this book. Evangelism in the style of Jesus; evangelism that flows like a dance.

Evangelism as dance begins with something beyond yourself. Think of a song that comes to you somehow from somewhere. At first you may catch only a note here, a phrase there, and it may sound strange. But once you really *hear* it, once you pick it up, once it finds its way into your soul and begins to play there, it feels so familiar, so natural, that you wonder if you have made it up yourself. Yet the song's splendor and grandeur and mystery convince you that its origin lies beyond your own imagination (even if imagination is the window by which it enters your soul). Your find yourself humming the song, tapping your finger to it, whistling it . . . and you wonder "Where did this come from? Who wrote this song? How did it get into my head?"

So the gospel comes to you not like a commercial on the radio or TV or a political slogan in a campaign or a scientific formula in a classroom, but like a song. It sneaks up on you, and then sneaks inside you. Somewhere in your journey through life, you begin to hear this song whose music captures your heart with its rhythm, melody, ambience, and glory, and you begin to move to its rhythm. Thus you enter the dance.

Over time, your whole life begins to harmonize to the song. Its rhythm awakens you; its tempo moves you, so you resonate with its tone and flow with its melody. The lyric gradually convinces you that the entire world was meant to share in this song with its message, its joy, its dance. If more people heard the music, their hatred would give way to reconciliation; their greed would melt into generosity; their grumbling would transform into gratitude; their mourning would be turned to dancing. People would stop polluting and start planting gardens, if they lived by the song. They would stop fighting and start playing hilarious practical jokes on each other, throwing joyous picnics and parties, playing raucous games, dreaming wild dreams, and enjoying a good laugh every chance they got.

This is why if you begin to feel the song and live by it, you desire to help others do the same for a number of reasons:

1. For the sheer beauty, truth, and goodness of the song. Something this wonderful must be shared.
2. For the good of your friends, neighbors, planet-mates who share the human predicament with you. As individuals,

their lives would be enriched if they heard the song and learned to move with it.

3. For the sake of the whole human race and the entire planet. If we humans don't learn to live by the beauty of the music, we'll live by our own destructive, greedy noise and despairing, consumptive silence, which will be disastrous for everyone and everything concerned.

4. For the sake of the composer, the singer, the player—the Triune God whose song rings in every note and every beat with a spirit of sharing.

Anyone who hears the song—truly hears it—must dance. And all dancers seek to share their joy. So let's talk about how. You are more ready for this than you realize. Get ready for something fresh, something new, something unexpected. Let's dance!

FOR FURTHER DISCUSSION

Why don't you invite a small group, class, or other circle of friends to read this book with you? Your agenda can be simple:

1. As you each read a chapter, underline words, phrases, or sentences of special interest, and write notes in the margins with your questions, comments, disagreements, and additional insights.

2. When you get together, share your underlinings and annotations. Just take turns answering these two simple questions: What is something in this chapter that struck you? Why?

3. After everyone shares, answer another group of questions: So what? What difference should what we have talked about make in the way we live, pray, relate, and serve? What will you apply to your life? What will you do differently, tomorrow or in the coming week or month, based on this reading and dialogue?

4. It would be a great ending if you turned your insights into simple, sincere prayers along these lines: "God, thank you for teaching us that..." or "God, help us to...."

1 | I Read Your Book This Morning

Shortly after the release of my second writing project, *Finding Faith*, I was invited to do a book signing at my church. It was an elegant affair, with a punch bowl (full of a bright red liquid, as I recall, but with a flavor hard to place) complete with a floating ring of something frozen and neon green, and silver trays of crumbly hors d'oeuvres—tasty, but messy, and too small to satisfy a hungry guy who didn't eat before coming. The final touch? The tasteful organizers had hired a talented harpist (a college student living near Washington D.C., but from Philadelphia) to provide delightful background music. After some informal socializing, I participated in an interview about the book (which gave the harpist a break—during which I happened to notice her leafing through a copy of my book), and then the music began and the small crowd returned to informal conversation.

At the end of the evening, I noticed the harpist struggling to load her harp into her van. (I secretly was thankful that I play the guitar, which is a lot easier to transport!) I offered to help her, and it wasn't easy. (Those harpists may look and sound as delicate as petite piccolo players, but they have to be stronger than tuba players!) After we closed the rear gate of her vehicle, she turned to me and with complete seriousness said, "While you were talking, I had a chance to look through your book. I have a question for you: Do you mean all that stuff you wrote in the book, or are you just trying to make Christianity sound good?"

I said, "Well, Alice (not her real name), that's quite a question! Tell me what you mean," and so began what I call a "spiritual friendship"—a friendship that continues to this day. I didn't actually see Alice for several months after that initial meeting, but I gave her a copy of my book, and within twenty-four hours I got the first of many emails, which I would like to share with you, with Alice's permission. I share them with you for a number of reasons:

1. So you can hear the real "voice" of an authentic spiritual seeker of a postmodern bent.
2. So you can begin to see how modern Christianity looks to a postmodern seeker.
3. So you can begin to imagine how you would have responded to Alice, to prepare yourself for some meaningful spiritual dialogues of your own.
4. So you can get a fresh vision of what evangelism should and can be.

I've maintained Alice's spelling and punctuation, and have only changed a few details for the sake of privacy. I hope you will find her messages as winsome, intriguing, stimulating, and challenging as I have.

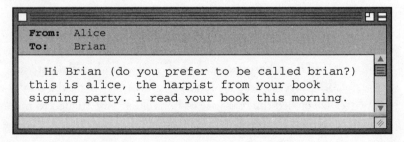

From: Alice
To: Brian

Hi Brian (do you prefer to be called brian?) this is alice, the harpist from your book signing party. i read your book this morning.

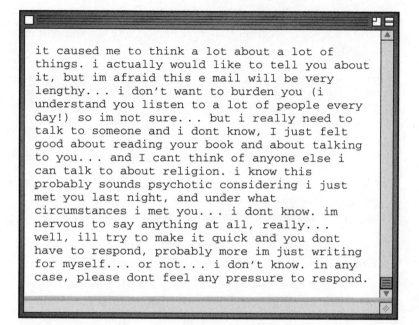

it caused me to think a lot about a lot of
things. i actually would like to tell you about
it, but im afraid this e mail will be very
lengthy... i don't want to burden you (i
understand you listen to a lot of people every
day!) so im not sure... but i really need to
talk to someone and i dont know, I just felt
good about reading your book and about talking
to you... and I cant think of anyone else i
can talk to about religion. i know this
probably sounds psychotic considering i just
met you last night, and under what
circumstances i met you... i dont know. im
nervous to say anything at all, really...
well, ill try to make it quick and you dont
have to respond, probably more im just writing
for myself... or not... i don't know. in any
case, please dont feel any pressure to respond.

"i read your book this morning." Doesn't that suggest a lot of
motivation to you? I hope the book is good, but I don't think I
can take credit for that kind of intense interest. And I don't think
Alice is alone in this intensity. All around me, all around you, are
people who would stay up half the night reading or talking if they
could get some help with their spiritual questions. All they need
is someone who cares and who has some spiritual experience and
wisdom to share. They are more ready than you realize—more
ready for a sincere spiritual friendship with someone like you.

I think you will agree that through this email Alice is doing her
part to establish a genuine friendship with me. She doesn't want
to burden me. She is careful not to be presumptuous, and doesn't
demand a response. (How different from some poor so-called

evangelists who talk whether or not others want to listen, and demand a response whether the other person is ready and willing or not.) She continues...

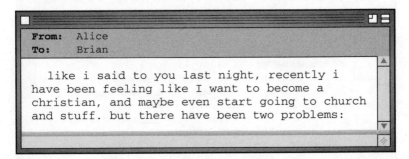

From: Alice
To: Brian

    like i said to you last night, recently i
have been feeling like I want to become a
christian, and maybe even start going to church
and stuff. but there have been two problems:

Before we get to the problems, notice this: As far as I can remember, Alice said nothing close to "I want to become a Christian." What she said was, "Do you really mean what you said in the book, or are you just trying to make Christianity sound good?" This is a reminder to us that what people mean is often different—and sometimes nearly opposite—of what they say. Underneath a criticism, underneath a seemingly negative statement, can be a test that says, "I really want to become a Christian, but first I must test you to see if you are a safe person to talk to. Will you react, get defensive, argue ... or listen?"

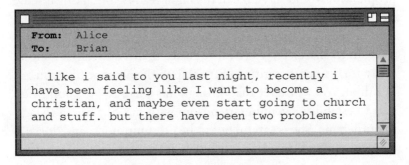

From: Alice
To: Brian

    like i said to you last night, recently i
have been feeling like I want to become a
christian, and maybe even start going to church
and stuff. but there have been two problems:

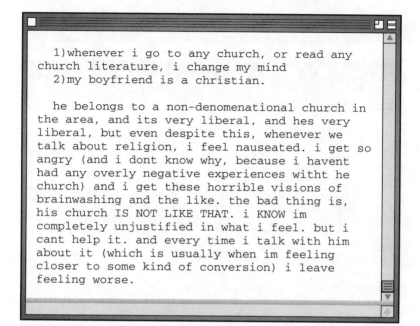

```
    1)whenever i go to any church, or read any
church literature, i change my mind
    2)my boyfriend is a christian.

    he belongs to a non-denomenational church in
the area, and its very liberal, and hes very
liberal, but even despite this, whenever we
talk about religion, i feel nauseated. i get so
angry (and i dont know why, because i havent
had any overly negative experiences witht he
church) and i get these horrible visions of
brainwashing and the like. the bad thing is,
his church IS NOT LIKE THAT. i KNOW im
completely unjustified in what i feel. but i
cant help it. and every time i talk with him
about it (which is usually when im feeling
closer to some kind of conversion) i leave
feeling worse.
```

There is a lot here for us to consider. Alice's line about changing her mind whenever she visits a church or reads Christian literature should give every pastor and Christian leader heartburn, if not a heart attack. You will also notice her use of the word *liberal*—by which, I think, she means contemporary and nontraditional, not "theologically liberal" in the technical sense. This reminds us not to assume that words have the same meanings to everyone. Church people develop complex and specialized lexicons that can be pretty off-putting to non-churchgoers. If we want to become spiritual friends to them, we need to start by not expecting them to conform to our vocabulary. As Christians, we live out a message about a man who came to us on our terms, spoke our language, and crossed the bridge to meet us where we were.

Angry, nauseated, horrible visions, brainwashing, worse—these are strong words and reveal intense feelings. She continues . . .

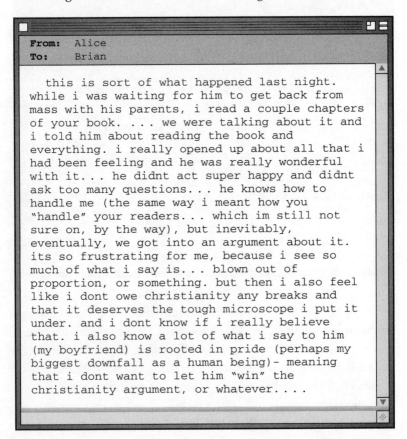

From: Alice
To: Brian

this is sort of what happened last night. while i was waiting for him to get back from mass with his parents, i read a couple chapters of your book. ... we were talking about it and i told him about reading the book and everything. i really opened up about all that i had been feeling and he was really wonderful with it... he didnt act super happy and didnt ask too many questions... he knows how to handle me (the same way i meant how you "handle" your readers... which im still not sure on, by the way), but inevitably, eventually, we got into an argument about it. its so frustrating for me, because i see so much of what i say is... blown out of proportion, or something. but then i also feel like i dont owe christianity any breaks and that it deserves the tough microscope i put it under. and i dont know if i really believe that. i also know a lot of what i say to him (my boyfriend) is rooted in pride (perhaps my biggest downfall as a human being)- meaning that i dont want to let him "win" the christianity argument, or whatever. . . .

Notice how her boyfriend was "really wonderful with it" when she began opening up about her spiritual interest: He "didn't act super happy and didn't ask too many questions." In other words, he gave her space. That is something we need to do for our spiritual friends. Can you see how it is possible for us to care too much—to care in such a way that we fail to give people the space they need?

And also notice how things went sour. True, she's willing to take a lot of responsibility for the argument that ensued (a rather humble act, admitting her pride as she did, don't you agree?). But more interesting is this: For her, the good news of Christianity keeps morphing into a "win-lose" affair, an argument. There is a lot we could say about this. For starters, we could talk about the whole career of modernity—where explorers were called *conquistadores* (conquerors)—where evangelistic initiatives were called *crusades,* like military invasions of conquest; where the Good News was phrased in terms of laws (who can argue against *laws?*) or steps (assembly instructions for a bicycle? What is to converse about there?) or simple diagrams (engineering schematics of the soul?). We could also talk about the language of "winning" people for Christ, a term with some biblical roots (1 Corinthians 9) to be sure, but in our modern competitive culture, our winning implies someone else's losing in a way that the image did not in ancient culture. Most productively, we could consider how in our rationalistic modern age, where "mind" is everything, the Christian gospel really has become an argument, and evangelism has located itself rhetorically somewhere between courtroom prosecution and door-to-door sales or cable TV infomercials, complete with clever closes ("Is there any reason, Mrs. Jones, why you *wouldn't* want to buy our new Dirt-B-Gone Household Vacuum System?").

For Jesus, there was indeed a time to argue. We see him in debate on many occasions with the religious leaders, for example. But have you ever noticed how "tricky" Jesus is in argument? Think of it like this ...

A   **B**

Let's say "A" represents the position of someone arguing against Jesus, and "B" represents the position this arguer expects Jesus to take. You can pick your issue ... divorce, punishing an immoral person, where true worship should occur, paying taxes to Caesar. But what does Jesus do? Does he respond to the force of A's position with even greater logic and persuasion for position B? No. Time and time again he asks a question or tells a story or in some other way slips out of position B altogether, and raises the whole line of discourse to a new level, moving to position C, as below.

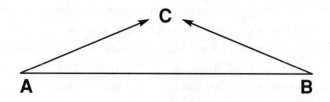

Why does he do this? Is it because he is "chicken"—afraid to lose, conflict-averse, too soft for a good-old-fashioned-knock-down-drag-out argument? You'd only ask that question if you didn't know much about Jesus. No, I think he transcends the normal lines of argument for several reasons, including these two:

1. Many arguments and questions are not framed in an acceptable way: They make assumptions that are not (from your perspective) valid. If you engage in the argument or answer the question as framed for you, you in a sense legitimize those invalid assumptions. For example, if someone asks you, "You're still drinking too much, aren't you?"—you can't respond to the "too much" and let the "still" stand as an assumption; that is, you can't if you have never, in fact, had the habit of drinking too much. Many times, Jesus will

not answer a question or respond to a provocative comment because the whole discussion is not framed in a wise or helpful or accurate way.

2. Sometimes when reading the Gospels, I sense that Jesus will not answer a question or engage in an argument because he does not want to humiliate his conversation partner. He finds a way to back down, to let the other person seem right or retain some dignity, rather than backing the person into a corner and proving, "No, you're wrong! I'm right! You lose! I win!" Jesus does this for reasons of gentleness and kindness and respect, and also for reasons of persuasion. He knows (as Alice does) that when you put people into a win-lose situation, when you don't give them space to think for themselves, they become less open, not more, to your ideas.

Needless to say, I think Alice is telling us something important: Evangelism in the postmodern world has to be less like an argument. This is not to say that it will not be logical, but rather that it will not be about winning and losing, which is why I think the image of dance works so well. Dance is not about winning and losing. When the music ends, you don't sneer at your partner and say, "Gotcha! I won that dance, 7 to 3!" And if you try to pull someone into a dance against her will, the term we use to describe that behavior is not "bold dancing," but rather "assault."

The great (and eccentric) Danish philosopher Søren Kierkegaard wrote one of the most intriguing books on evangelism ever written (in my also somewhat eccentric opinion), called *The Point of View for My Work as an Author: A Report to History.* (In fact, I would put it, along with an article by American novelist Walker Percy called "The Message in the Bottle," at the very top of writings that have stimulated me to think about evangelism in new ways.) Kierkegaard uses a metaphor even more unexpected than dance to describe the kind of evangelism needed in his day. He claims that the evangelist is like a person who hides behind a bush, and when his friend walks by, he sneaks up behind him and gives him a kick in the backside (Kierkegaard uses a more graphic term). Then, he dives behind the bush again. His friend turns around and sees no one and then continues walking. But as he walks, he is no longer walking along semiconscious. He is startled, scratching his head, looking around, and wondering, "Who was that? What's going on here? Am I being watched?" His whole mind and curiosity are awakened.

In a similar way, when a person helps another person begin to think about spiritual matters, he dives behind a bush. He "doesn't act super happy about it" or ask too many questions, but rather he hides, to give his friend space, time, and privacy to think through these matters on his own. Kierkegaard also uses the metaphor of being a midwife, a metaphor borrowed from Socrates. The evangelist is never coercive, pushy, combative; rather, she is patient and gentle like a midwife, knowing that the giving of life takes time and cannot be rushed without potentially lethal damage.

Closed-Minded and Bigoted and Brainwashed and Everything Bad

Alice is onto something we should think about ourselves: Evangelism should be about relationships (what we are calling spiritual friendships), not arguments. She continues:

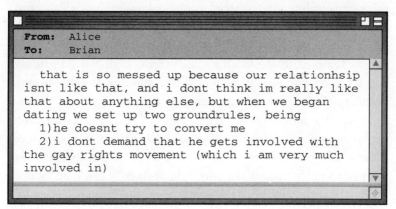

From: Alice
To: Brian

that is so messed up because our relationhsip
isnt like that, and i dont think im really like
that about anything else, but when we began
dating we set up two groundrules, being
1)he doesnt try to convert me
2)i dont demand that he gets involved with
the gay rights movement (which i am very much
involved in)

Can you see how "trying to convert" someone is inconsistent with a relationship? It is wrestling, not dancing; an argument, not conversation; win-lose, not win-win; sales and conquest, not friendship.

Can you see how sincere Christians so often self-sabotage evangelism, especially when they talk about issues like homosexuality?

Alice's comments make this so clear. For many conservative Christians here in the United States, homosexuality has become more than a difficult moral and social question—it has become a line in the sand, turf upon which a political power struggle occurs, a symbol of the loss of cultural dominance, a kind of moral "last straw." It is like a line of scrimmage in a football game that we are losing. Our quarterback has been sacked for three consecutive downs. First we were on the opponent's twenty-yard line, but we lost thirty yards on the issue of separation of church and state, when we were no longer able to have our kind of prayer in public schools. That put us at midfield, but then we lost another twenty yards on the issues of abortion and divorce. Our front line tried to stop these issues from encroaching, but we collapsed under a blitz and experienced another sack. Then our offensive line tried to stand strong one more time, so we could throw a long pass and regain lost yardage through political control via "the religious right," but our opponent rushed in from the left and we fumbled, losing another fifteen yards, leaving us at the fourth and long, on our own fifteen-yard line, the line of opposition to homosexuality. Surely we can't give up any more yardage!

Ironically, for the other team, homosexuality is every bit as moral an issue as it is for conservative Christians, but for a completely different reason. (If conservative Christians listened long enough to really understand this, I think their "game plan" would change dramatically.) For the other team, the game has gone like this: First, the opponents tried to gain ground on slavery, but our valiant defense rushed and sacked them on that one. Then, they tried to score on the continued disenfranchisement of women—first not allowing them to vote, then not allowing them to make personal decisions about reproduction, and also refusing to pay them fairly as compared to men—but we managed to sack them again. Then, they tried to maintain their religious privilege and dominance over us through "blue laws" (laws restricting Sunday activities) and school prayer, but again we penetrated their front line and they lost yardage. Now, they're still trying to defend immoral and outdated ways by treating homosexuals in the same unjust and uncompassionate ways they used to treat blacks and women and Jews. They've been defeated in their injustice in the past, and we can't let them turn the tide now.

Do you see how the same issue looks so different, depending on which side of the line of scrimmage you are standing? No wonder Alice is careful to stay out of a combative, competitive, win-lose mode. She rightly knows that matters of the spirit cannot be decided by coercion—physical, political, or even interpersonal. In this, of course, she is echoing both Paul and Peter in the New Testament.

> The Lord's servant must not quarrel; instead, he must be kind to everyone, able to teach, not resentful. Those who oppose him he must gently instruct, in the hope that God will grant them repentance, leading them to a knowledge of the truth, and that they will come to their senses.... (2 Timothy 2:24–26)

> Always be prepared to give an answer to everyone who asks you to give the reason for the hope that you have. But do this with gentleness and respect.... (1 Peter 3:15)

Alice continues:

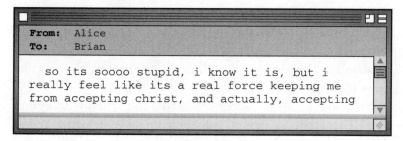

```
From:   Alice
To:     Brian

   so its soooo stupid, i know it is, but i
really feel like its a real force keeping me
from accepting christ, and actually, accepting
```

god. when i was reading your book today at
certain parts i felt so good, and at certain
times i actually felt like i was about to cry,
because it felt like something was really
getting through to me. but i feel like theres
something holding me back, theres some sort of
defense mechanism in me that tells me not to
believe any of it. i guess thats probably why i
asked you what i did last night. i need to make
sure that im not being "lured in", just to find
out once i go ahead and believe that a whole
bunch of other stuff comes along with it that
i cant feel comfortable with, and then my whole
person will change and ill become closed minded
and bigoted and brainwashed and everything
bad. . . i just cant feel that i can trust it.
i dont know what to do.
  oh well. at the very least, i really enjoyed
reading your book. i thought it was really funny
(in a good way) and really insightful, and it
was clear you really understood how a persons
mind in that situation works. it met me at every
corner. that was frustrating, in a way, but in a
healthy way, like eating veggies or soemthing.
ill try to write a review of it online when i
get a chance. hope you had a good easter.
  alice

I remember originally reading this part of Alice's first email to
me and thinking, Wow, that original question wasn't just a casual
conversation opener. It was a well-thought-out expression of her
attraction and revulsion to the Christian faith. Several things strike
me in these paragraphs.

First, she speaks of "accepting christ, and actually, accepting
god." This language (which will come up again in a later email)

reminds me that the doctrine of the Trinity, which we Christians take for granted, creates a lot of confusion for the average spiritual seeker. For the original followers of Christ, of course, there was no "doctrine of the Trinity." There was simply this charismatic and enigmatic character named Jesus, whose message was compelling and whose presence was radiant with the goodness and glory of God. As the centuries have passed, the church has of necessity developed various doctrines, in most cases, to correct tendencies toward gross misunderstandings of the essential Christian faith. However, as the centuries pass, the bulk of doctrines accumulates, like a tugboat taking barge after barge in tow as it moves upriver, and eventually, the weight of the barges plus the strength of the opposing current makes progress impossible.

We have to find ways for people to simply encounter Christ—and God too!—without having to figure out two millennia of church history, controversy, and dogma. How will we find those ways? This is a major question for our best theologians to wrestle with as we enter Christianity's third millennium. For what it's worth, here is my proposal: We have to re-root doctrine in the Christian story. Instead of presenting our doctrines as abstractions floating out in space, we must show how the various articulations of Christian belief arose in the context of Christianity's spread, its inevitable experience of controversy, and the contrary influences from the various cultures and philosophies, which the gospel encountered and engaged.

Of course, Alice does not mention any of this complexity, but I think you will agree that her language of "accepting christ, and actually, accepting god" suggests that in order to be good spiritual friends, we should help clear up confusion, not add to it. We can accomplish this by keeping things simple, by focusing on the essentials of understanding and issues appropriate for our friends' current needs and by realizing that spiritual seekers are not going to get the whole range of Christian theology in one package.

Here is one way I try to explain "accepting christ, and actually, accepting god." I try to explain to people that just as Jesus wants to lead people to God, God also wants to lead people to Jesus. Why? That question is best answered with a question: What is God like? The answer to that question depends on whom you ask. It is fascinating (but then again, not all that surprising) how people tend to describe God as a bigger and better version of themselves. So for the conservatives, God is conservative (surprise!); for the liberals, God is liberal; for intellectuals, God is clothed in abstractions and complexities; while for the uneducated, God is a down-to-earth and simple kind of guy. For the military man, God tends to be about power; while for the bureaucrat, God is about policies. For the artist, God has a wildness and beauty that inspires and attracts; while for the engineer, God's grandeur is in predictability, stability, definition— opposite qualities from those loved by the artist. For the social worker, God sides with the poor and oppressed; while for the entrepreneur, God rewards the diligent and clever. The chauvinist's God is strong, virile, male; if you ask the feminist about God, he or she will tell you, "Well, first of all, She is...." We could telescope this out to larger perspectives too—how the Western view of God reflects Western sensibilities, the Eastern reflects Eastern, and views of tribal cultures and subcultures reflect their own distinct views.

Now, imagine you are God. (If this comes easy for you, we should all be worried!) What do You do about all these versions of You, made in human images? Of course there is an element of truth in nearly everyone's image of You. But on the other hand, each has its distortions, its imbalances, its gaps, its excesses, its voids. (For example, the god of the racist or chauvinist tends to share the biases of its worshipers.) So, what if You decided to pour

Yourself into a human being who would walk into the middle of all the projections and expectations people have created to explicate You, and in this person You embodied a true, full, dynamic, pure, and undomesticated image of Yourself? If You were to do that, wouldn't You want to lead people—from Jewish shepherds in their fields to "pagan" Eastern astrologers (as the Christmas story recounts), from prostitutes to priests, from military generals to political revolutionaries, from blue-collar fishermen to white-collar scholars (as the Gospels recount)—to this person, so they could get a balanced and accurate and inspiring window into Your heart, mind, and being? This is one way I try to explain how "accepting Christ" relates to "accepting God."

Back to Alice's comments. Listen to her again:

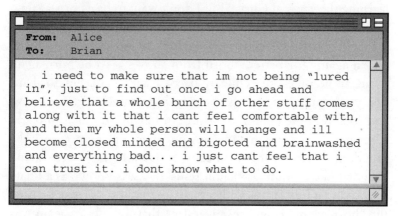

From: Alice
To: Brian

i need to make sure that im not being "lured in", just to find out once i go ahead and believe that a whole bunch of other stuff comes along with it that i cant feel comfortable with, and then my whole person will change and ill become closed minded and bigoted and brainwashed and everything bad. . . i just cant feel that i can trust it. i dont know what to do.

Do you feel the legitimacy of Alice's fear about her "whole person" changing? We Christians often talk about changed lives, but we fail to see that to many of our neighbors, the changes that occur with conversion are not all for the good. An example of this is Dan, who began attending church with my son, Brett, in high school. One summer, Dan went on vacation with our family. Brett, Dan, and I were driving somewhere in the car (actually, we were going to explore a rattlesnake den, but that's another story), and I asked him, "Where are you these days in your relationship with God?"

Dan replied, "Mr. McLaren, coming to church has really helped me. All I really want now is to learn the ways of Christ."

I remember thinking, *"Ways of Christ" . . . that's a great way of saying it.*

Then he continued: "But one thing: I hope I never become a born-again." I asked him why that was, and he answered, "A friend of ours at school became a born-again. She used to be a really nice person, but now she's always judging everybody and she's pushed away all of her friends. It's like either they have to convert, or she doesn't want them as a friend. So I want to keep learning the ways of Christ, but I don't want to be a born-again."

No doubt, what Dan meant by "learning the ways of Christ" is exactly what Jesus meant in John 3 when he talked about being "born again" (or better, "born from above"). To be born again means to become like a child, to become a learner again, to abandon your adult pretensions about how much you already know, and to accept the childlike posture of having so much to learn. Elsewhere, Jesus said that this posture opens one's entrée into the kingdom of God. Most ironically, to Dan, being "born again" sounded like becoming what in Jesus' day was known as a Pharisee . . . and oddly, it was with a Pharisee that Jesus originally used the "born again" language, suggesting that to be born again was the opposite of being a Pharisee!

I wonder how many people are out there like Alice and Dan, who would like to become Christians, but are afraid it will make them into worse (i.e. less tolerant and loving, less forgiving, less open and friendly, less honest and authentic, less human and humble) people, not better.

A fellow named Jeff began attending my church, and after about six months he told me, "For the first time in my life, I look forward to coming to church. It's really having a good effect on me and my whole family. My wife says I'm a much better husband, and I know I'm improving as a father too. I really get a lot out of your sermons. In fact, I agree with everything you say." That statement shocked me, since my wife couldn't even say that . . . nor could I, since I often wince when listening to old sermon tapes! But then he continued, "There's one thing, though. I don't believe in God."

Inside, of course, I'm wondering, *How can you agree with everything I say but not believe in God? Some preacher I am!* But instead I asked him, "Why don't you believe in God?" (An essential element of good spiritual friendship—something I'm learning from Jesus—is knowing which questions are helpful and which aren't.)

Jeff answered, "It's my brother. He became a Christian and now nobody can stand him."

I asked, "So you're afraid that if you start believing in God, you'll become an arrogant hypocrite, or something like that?"

"Exactly."

I felt I should just give him something to think about, rather than argue (remember, it is not about winning and losing), so I said, "Well, maybe someday you'll see a way to believe in God and become a better person instead of a worse one."

He said, "Wow, I never really thought of it that way. I guess that is an option." It took a few months, but eventually he got beyond his fear and became a growing follower of Christ.

What elements of Alice's email strike you the most? In what ways can you agree with her? What would you have said in reply to this message?

3 | Three Realizations

As I reflect on Alice's first email, along with hundreds of other conversations with spiritual seekers like her, several conclusions begin to form in my thinking.

1. Many people want to talk about God, but not just anybody is safe to talk to.

I remember in high school, a new Christian myself, hearing that Monica had become a Christian over Easter vacation. This surprised me, as Monica was a beautiful and popular cheerleader with a reputation of hanging out with a pretty wild crowd. But rumor had it that she had visited relatives over Easter and had "gotten saved." I sought her out and cautiously asked her if the rumors were true. They were, she assured me, and told me that "everyone" knew I was a Christian and so she was looking forward to getting to know me and having me introduce her to some other Christians. Then she told me something that I didn't expect to hear. "You know, the whole crowd I hang out with . . . all of them are thinking about God. A lot of times even when we're drinking or getting high, we talk all night about God and our beliefs and our doubts and stuff."

Now years later, I wonder why none of them felt safe coming to me, since "everyone" knew I was a Christian. I think they sensed—

and they were probably right back then—that if they approached me, I would push too hard and not give them space. I wouldn't have been a spiritual friend, but rather a spiritual salesman. For me back then, evangelism was still too much wrestling match, not enough dance.

So here we are, with two unacceptable alternatives. On the one hand, we have safe people who don't have much to offer their friends spiritually, and on the other, we have spiritually knowledgeable people who aren't safe to talk to, because they will come on too strong. Can you see why I feel we have to create a new term like "spiritual friendship" to try to explore a third option—becoming a friend (not a salesman) who is truly spiritual, safe to talk to, and worth talking to? That is why people often test us with seemingly hostile statements, like Alice's "Do you really believe what you say, or are you just trying to make Christianity look good?" If we respond argumentatively, or in some other inauthentic way, we disqualify ourselves as a spiritual friend.

2. You have to see, like, approach, and serve people if you want to become their spiritual friend.

The fact that I noticed Alice struggling with her harp and went over to help her with it gave her the chance to begin a conversation. If I hadn't done so, chances are she would have gone home with the question turning in her mind with no one to ask. Some people call it "earning the right to be heard"—by serving, listening, caring, smiling, or doing something to show yourself a friendly person, a potentially safe person.

One of my favorite churches is Vineyard Christian Fellowship in Cincinnati. They are famous for something called "servant evangelism." They invite church members to go out to serve the community by providing free gift wrapping during the Christmas season, by going door-to-door in apartments in poor parts of town to check and replace batteries in smoke detectors, by cleaning toilets in public buildings and restaurants, by throwing parties for the homeless. These deeds of service help the receivers in many practical ways, no doubt, but I think there is an equal or greater benefit for those who go out from the church to serve: It teaches them that to be a Christian means to be *a servant.* Not a know-it-all, not a door-to-door free-ticket-to-heaven salesperson, not a moral police officer or scolding elementary school teacher, not a bring-along-a-guilty-conscience, but a servant.

This servant identity goes to the heart of what is probably the greatest heresy in the history of monotheism. As I have written in *Finding Faith,* the greatest enemy to monotheism is not pantheism or atheism or polytheism, rather it is bad monotheism. Probably it is this heresy that is the defining characteristic of bad monotheism. What is the heresy? That to be one of God's people means to be chosen for exclusive and elite privilege, not universal service and sacrifice. If you go back to the beginning of Jewish identity, you find Abraham receiving this command and promise from God:

> Leave your country, your people, and your father's household and go to the land I will show you. I will make you into a great nation and I will bless you; I will make your name great, and you will be a blessing. I will bless those who bless you, and whoever curses you I will curse; and all peoples on earth will be blessed through you."
> (Genesis 12:1–3)

The command launches Abraham on a journey, and God's people have been on a journey ever since. The journey is a journey of blessing, to be sure, but it is *not* an elite and exclusive blessing. Rather, God's people are blessed *instrumentally*—blessed in order to be a blessing to *others*. The way God blesses everyone is by blessing some and giving them the role of servants to bless everyone else. The prophets echo this theme—they fight against the gravity of spiritual selfishness and religious exclusivism until Jesus comes "in the fullness of time" to bring the Jewish blessing to the whole world. Without this servant identity truly and deeply ingrained in us, I do not think anything we do can be truly called *evangelism,* because *evangelism* means "spreading good news," and as non-servants, our elitist identity will pollute our message so that our version of the news becomes less than good. As servants we can bear good news whether we help a new acquaintance load a harp into a van, listen to a stranger's problems, or devote a year of our lives to bringing clean water to a North African village. We can spread the Good News by seeing ourselves not as a privileged, chosen, exclusive elite, but as people called and then sent to be servants to all, following the example of Jesus, who repeatedly said, "I have not come to be served, but to serve."

3. Many people have stayed away from Christianity for good reasons.

As I reflect on Alice's insights, I realize that part of the revulsion of some people has to do with them loving their selfishness, sexual promiscuity, arrogance, racism, resentments, self-righteousness, and materialism so much that they want to stay far from anything that will challenge or threaten their status quo. But much of the revulsion to Christianity in many people is trying to tell us something about ourselves as Christians, something that we don't want to hear but need to hear: (1) our faith has too often become for us just another rigid belief system instead of a unique, joyful way of living, loving, and serving; (2) our concern for getting our own and others' souls into heaven after we die has too often seduced us into neglecting our call to seek justice and mercy here and now on this earth; and (3) faith has too often become for us a set of easy answers and cardboard explanations instead of a window into unfathomable mystery and a pathway into an awesome adventure.

In all of these ways and more, Alice's first message got me thinking. . . .

4 | Err . . . I'll Deal With It Later

Some time later, I received this second message from Alice:

From: Alice
To: Brian

   hi brian, sorry its taken me so long to write
back. i wanted to wait until i had something
specific to say. i still dont. im not feeling
the same drastic pull i was feeling a little
while ago towards god. its frustrating and i
have so much going on in my life right now that
often I just push it out of my head and say
"err... ill deal with it later." thats no good,
i know, and i wish i could just believe in god.
i like the idea of it, i like the feeling i get
when i feel like i do believe.
   I like the security of faith. but i just cant
seem to bring it on. i cant really pray anymore,
either, and thats frustrating. it sounds
ridiculous to say that i cant pray, but thats
what it is. i used to pray all the time, even
after i rejected a lot of what i was shown of
christianity. sometime last semester, it stopped
being sincere. i just didn't feel like i could
connect with god anymore. ive been thinking

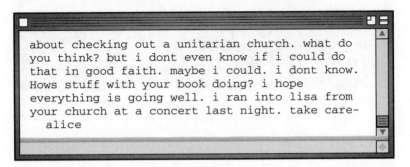

about checking out a unitarian church. what do
you think? but i dont even know if i could do
that in good faith. maybe i could. i dont know.
Hows stuff with your book doing? i hope
everything is going well. i ran into lisa from
your church at a concert last night. take care-
  alice

Alice's admission that her pull toward God ebbs and flows is refreshingly honest, isn't it? So does mine, actually. Also interesting is the fact that she used to pray "all the time," even after rejecting a lot of what she was shown of Christianity. If we are going to be effective spiritual friends, we need to realize that there is a lot of prayer going on "out there." Sometimes I think there is more prayer out there than in the church. That fact tells us something important: Our job as spiritual friends is seldom to get a fire started from scratch. Usually, we come into lives where there is already a candle burning—a flicker of prayer, a glow of faith, a flame of spiritual desire. Rather than critiquing the flame for being inconstant and flickering, we should seek to honor it for glowing at all, and try to fan the ember into a brighter, warmer, and stronger flame.

Why do you think Alice is considering a Unitarian church? Might it be because a Unitarian church is one of the few places where it is okay to have and discuss spiritual questions, doubts, and frustrations without being pressured to "get fixed" fast? (I know, there can be an opposite problem in some churches, Unitarian and otherwise, that when one begins to find something or Someone to believe in, one no longer fits in.) How could all our churches become safer places for seekers to seek, and still remain safe places for those who have found a life-giving connection with God to grow in their faith?

Also, why do you think Alice does not consider coming to the church I pastor? I have never asked her this, but I wonder if maybe she values our emerging friendship to such a degree that she does not want it to be compromised by pastor-parishioner complications. I remember how some other friends, both confessed agnostics but intrigued by an approach to faith that seemed "intelligent" to them, once told me, "Brian, we love you and your wife so much. We would like to visit your church, but we value our friendship so much we are afraid attending your church would somehow hurt our friendship." I could see their point. I don't have a solution to this problem, but I think it is enough for now to realize how rare and precious spiritual friendships are to spiritual seekers—they deserve protection.

Whatever her reasons for not attending my church, in thinking about finding a church, Alice is realizing something important: The search for God requires solitude, but it also requires community. People need a community where they can seek God in an encouraging context. I was hoping she would visit our church sometime, but I was careful not to push. I had to trust that she would be interested in coming in her own time. As her next email makes clear, going to church sometimes can lead to setbacks, not breakthroughs.

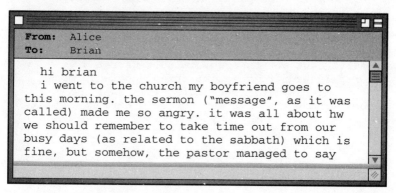

From: Alice
To: Brian

hi brian
  i went to the church my boyfriend goes to this morning. the sermon ("message", as it was called) made me so angry. it was all about hw we should remember to take time out from our busy days (as related to the sabbath) which is fine, but somehow, the pastor managed to say

that christians shouldnt date or marry non-
christians and its christians responsibility to
tell sinners and non-christians what they are
doing wrong and to lead them to Jesus. He was
saying that the "sinners" would be thankful
they were told what they were doing wrong... i
was like, man, who are you kidding? it's like
that Neitzche quote in your book "It would be
easier to believe in Christ if it weren't for
the Christians..." or whatever the exact quote
was. its confusing for me because ive seen a
lot of evidence supporting the fact that this
church is pretty open-minded, its definitely
very diverse and has seemed really accepting.
But that just makes me so much more scared
about jumping in and believing, like all the
good things i think about christianity are just
an illusion im creating or being shown and then
after i believe and put my heart into it i wont
have a choice but to conform to everything that
constitutes being a christian in reality. does
that make sense? its a lot like the first
question i asked you about your book, wondering
if you were just saying it to get people to
believe or if what you wrote really was true.
am i too obsessed with details?

why is it so easy for some people to swallow
all of this? the pastor at this church today
was saying how when people want to believe in
God, "he" makes it easy for them and they're
welcomed with open arms. why doesnt it feel
like that for me? i feel like theres a huge
wall i cant get through. im so frustrated.
i really want to be a christian and feel good
about it. why is it so difficult? (sorry, i
dont expect you to answer these questions, im
just kind of letting my mind wander.) ugh...
its been a rough semester. take care-
    alice

In the email before this one, Alice had said that she was losing interest, but it is clear here that the intensity has returned. There is an important lesson here in spiritual friendship: Sometimes it is more important to keep the conversation going than to resolve every issue that arises. I suppose we faith-sharers need faith—faith that God is working in the person's life from many directions; faith that it is not all up to me and that it does not all depend on this one friendship; faith that God will not give up on the person; faith that God's Spirit is so pervasive that even after desire recedes, it will resurge again.

Of course, the intensity is shown here by anger, frustration, and disappointment. And no wonder! The pastor's "message" about not marrying or dating non-Christians must have felt like a direct assault on her relationship to her boyfriend. The pastor also appeared to be encouraging the very caricature that Alice is afraid of becoming—someone who is always telling "sinners" where they are wrong. Furthermore, he claimed that believing is easy ... but that is not how it feels for Alice. Her natural question is "Why doesn't it feel like that for me?" But do you feel the questions hidden behind it: "Is there something wrong with me? Or is there something wrong with this preacher for making everything sound so easy?" No wonder she found it all hard to "swallow."

But do you feel the glimmer of desire in this frustration, especially when she says, "I really want to be a Christian and feel good about it"? Alice gives an important insight into real spiritual friendship when she says, "I don't expect you to answer these questions. I'm just kind of letting my mind wander." I think she actually means, "I don't *want* you to answer these questions. I just want you to listen, to be present, to keep me company through this search," which is what I tried to do.

Notice what, for Alice, marked authenticity in the church she visited: It was *open-minded, diverse, accepting*. How would you put those characteristics into your own words? Do you think your church would be a better church if it were more open-minded, diverse, and accepting? Why do you think these qualities are so important to Alice and to contemporary people in general? Do you see any resonance between those qualities and any teachings of Jesus? Why do you believe so many churches seem closed-minded, homogenous, and judgmental?

Perhaps you are familiar with the term *apologetics,* which is the study of how to give a reasonable defense for the Christian faith. I wonder sometimes, especially since "defense" implies warfare rather than friendship, if postmodern apologetics should take a different approach. Instead of defending, perhaps apologetics should begin with an old-fashioned apology: *I'm sorry we Christians have so often put roadblocks up for spiritual seekers through our narrow-mindedness, our failure to bridge racial and cultural and class barriers, and our lack of acceptance. I'm sincerely sorry. Please don't blame Jesus for our failure to live up to his teaching and example. And be assured that we'll try to do better, with God's help. Please pray for us, okay?*

Before we go on, reread the sentences following "But that just makes me so much more scared..." and ask yourself if you can really understand what Alice is saying and feeling. Ask yourself how you would respond to that message. Apparently (again, I'm sorry I didn't save my replies), I responded to her email with a question. This is another reminder that one of the most important skills of spiritual friendship is learning to respond to questions with more questions, not answers, just as Jesus did so often. Alice came back with this:

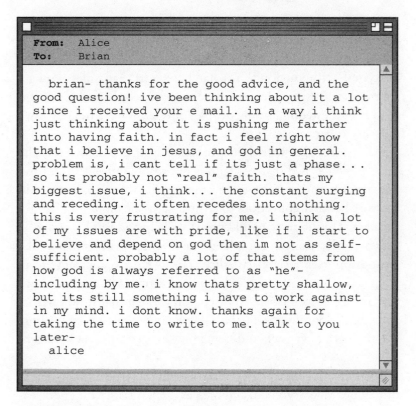

From: Alice
To: Brian

brian- thanks for the good advice, and the good question! ive been thinking about it a lot since i received your e mail. in a way i think just thinking about it is pushing me farther into having faith. in fact i feel right now that i believe in jesus, and god in general. problem is, i cant tell if its just a phase... so its probably not "real" faith. thats my biggest issue, i think... the constant surging and receding. it often recedes into nothing. this is very frustrating for me. i think a lot of my issues are with pride, like if i start to believe and depend on god then im not as self-sufficient. probably a lot of that stems from how god is always referred to as "he"-including by me. i know thats pretty shallow, but its still something i have to work against in my mind. i dont know. thanks again for taking the time to write to me. talk to you later-
    alice

Alice makes it clear why questions are often so much more valuable than answers: "just thinking about it is pushing me farther into having faith." There are a thousand forces in our lives pushing us away from "thinking about it"—forces saying, "Buy this product! Anesthetize yourself! Focus on your body; forget your soul! Impress other people; forget about God! Seek power, pleasure, prestige, not God!" Spiritual friends, wherever they go, are gentle and persistent agents working against these contrary forces, patiently helping people to keep "thinking about it."

You will notice that "jesus, and god in general" comes up again. How do the two go together? For some people, it seems that Jesus is not the way to God, but rather he is *in* the way to God, as if he is saying, "No you don't! You can't come to God unless you get by me first!" Again, Jesus is here to help people find God, and God is interested in leading people to Jesus. What a tragedy if we give any other impression!

Alice struggles with two problems in this email. First, she remains concerned that her faith is not real because it surges and recedes. Of course, if you were her spiritual friend, you could reassure her that yours does too—it is faith one minute and doubt the next. This honesty would probably help her. But I wonder . . . do you really want to completely resolve this problem? Isn't the frustration itself a sign that Alice wants a steady, constant, deep, stable faith? Isn't that a good desire to affirm and celebrate, not just a tension to relieve? And wouldn't it help her to know that sometimes doubt is actually holy—when it reveals a desire to pursue the truth, even when doing so means revising one's current beliefs?

Secondly, Alice struggles with referring to God as "he." She is not alone: Many women, and men as well, resist (with good reason, in my opinion) the idea of God as an "alpha male" on whom one must depend. That kind of dependence, they fear, only serves to reinforce a kind of weakness and ugly dependence in believers, while bolstering a chauvinistic worldview that places maleness on top of the "great chain of being." This is a huge subject, easily deserving a book in itself. (I devoted a single chapter to it in *Finding Faith*, but apparently that chapter did not help her a great deal. . . .) But the very least a spiritual friend can do for someone like Alice is to understand the reasons for her struggle, and assure her that there were good reasons for biblical language using predominantly, though not exclusively, male imagery for God (I mention some of these in *Finding Faith*), and assure her that God's true essence both comprises and transcends the virtues we associate with both maleness and femaleness.

When I answered Alice's email, I offered this observation: Maybe many of her problems arise from the fact that the version of Christianity that has been presented to her has been expressed in exclusively modern thoughts, while she is a postmodern person. Maybe, if she were to hear the Christian message presented in more postmodern terms and thoughts, she could "believe and feel good about it."

That idea seemed to make sense to her, as you will see in her next message.

5 | The Modern View of Christianity vs. the Postmodern View

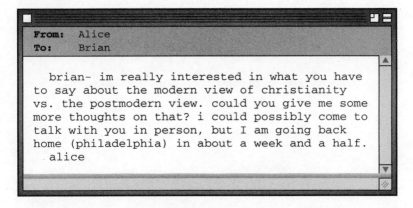

From: Alice
To: Brian

brian- im really interested in what you have to say about the modern view of christianity vs. the postmodern view. could you give me some more thoughts on that? i could possibly come to talk with you in person, but I am going back home (philadelphia) in about a week and a half.
 alice

If I were to sum up what I have learned about evangelism from Alice and so many people like her in the last ten years, here is what I would say: *Postmodern people don't want a God shrunken to fit modern tastes.* Unfortunately, the only God most of us have to offer postmoderns is a thoroughly modernized one. This fact is surprising in a way because the Bible is not a modern text by any stretch of the imagination, and the God of the Bible wears neither the three-piece suit nor the lab coat of modernity.

But then again, our "modernization" of God is not that surprising because through the sermons of preachers like me (not just on

Sundays, but through the "miracle" of radio and TV, sermons are as ubiquitous these days as commercials for Pepsi or Honda), we filter and revise—I am tempted to say "distort," but I won't—the image of God found in Scripture into acceptably modern categories.

Now please understand that by "modern" I do not mean contemporary. By modern, I mean a broad, coherent culture in Western civilization, arising (more or less) in the sixteenth century and developing through the twentieth, a culture dominated by science, consumerism, conquest, rationalism, mechanism, analysis, and objectivity. Is it such a great surprise or scandal that our image of God would gradually conform to our own tastes, so God would become our kind of winner (conquering everyone through logical argument or verbal intimidation): scientific, rationalistic, objective (expressing himself in absolute principles, propositions, formulae, facts, like any good scientist), and consumeristic (offering us blessings as commodities for our personal pleasure and individual advancement)?

I have mixed feelings about the modernization of our concept of God. Obviously, God is not less than these modern values, so we can thank modernity for elevating our concept of God where our premodern concepts were, perhaps, inferior. But here is the problem: What if God is still more than these modern concepts can contain, the way a poet's language is in a sense more than that of an engineer or scientist, or the way an opera or painting is more than a formula or diagram? And what if our modern depictions of God seem to postmodern people to limit and constrict their imagination about God, rather than inspire it to new heights?

Again, this is a subject deserving a whole book (my *A New Kind of Christian* [Jossey-Bass, 2001] is an early run into this territory, as is *The Church on the Other Side* [Zondervan, 2000]). But even better than reading a book is engaging in spiritual friendship with people like Alice, because their stubborn refusal to be content with our modern depiction of God will push us better than any book could to realize that God is not limited to our modern conceptualizations. In this way, engaging in spiritual friendship will not only help others become Christians, it will help us become better Christians, who love God more than ever. This occurs because our concept of God is expanding, deepening, and growing more glorious through conversation with our seeking friends. In essence, the Christians are "converted" first in authentic spiritual friendships.

There is a wonderful story in the New Testament that prepares us for this kind of profound transformation in ourselves as "converted" people who seek to help our as-yet-"unconverted" friends. As you read the story found in Acts 10:1–11:18, be careful not to reconfigure it to fit into your preexisting categories. Try to let it stretch or even deconstruct your current categories. As I read it, here is what I find:

There is a man named Cornelius who is neither Christian nor Jew, but he is a God-fearing Roman guy, a man a lot like Alice in the way he tries to do good and he prays a lot, even though he is an outsider to established religion. One afternoon he receives a vision of an angel. The angel says that God has noticed his prayers and good deeds. Oddly, the angel does not give him the message he needs, but rather tells him how to make contact with a man named Peter, who can give him that message. (Could this angelic reticence in itself be a message for us? Is the good news supposed to spread through human-to-human relationships, exactly the kinds of spiritual friendships we are talking about in this book, and that these relationships are an even better vehicle than more "supernatural" revelations, such as an angelic vision?)

Shortly after Cornelius receives one vision, Peter is receiving another, an odd one involving a crazy command by God to do what

Peter feels is sin. How could God tempt Peter to sin? Through this disturbing and bizarre vision/dream of what we would call cognitive and moral dissonance, Peter is prepared to rethink his categories—just in time for an invitation by Cornelius's servants to come to visit Cornelius in his own home some distance away.

When Peter arrives, Cornelius is so moved that he falls down at Peter's feet in reverence, but Peter can't accept this show of respect. He puts himself on common ground with Cornelius, setting the stage for a mutual relationship—an authentic spiritual friendship—by saying, "Stand up. I am only a man myself."

"Only a man [or human being] myself"—that is good mental health, and a good posture of spiritual friendship. So many of us feel unqualified to be active spiritual friends because we don't feel *spiritual*—we feel so *human*. But Peter shows us here that being human is what it is all about. When I think about the power of our humanness, I think about a friend of mine, Robert, a fellow pastor who has an extraordinary (and sometimes a bit *devilish*) sense of humor.

As I recall hearing the story, Robert was vacationing in Orlando, Florida, with his family. After a long day of standing in long lines (in my experience, the unattractive main activity at Orlando's so-called "attractions"), the family was too exhausted to go out for dinner. So Robert went to a Chinese carry-out near their hotel. While waiting in yet another line, he noticed the woman in front of him had an Australian accent. He struck up a friendly conversation with her and learned a lot about her. She and her husband were both photographers, had three children, and were celebrating their fifteenth anniversary. Then they both ordered for their families, and Rob took a walk around the parking lot while waiting for his food to be prepared and packed into those little white cardboard containers.

When he came back, there was a line again, this time waiting to pick up and pay for orders. This time, he noticed a tall fellow in front of him with an Australian accent. Rob got an idea (maybe it should be called a *temptation*) he could not resist. He began to talk to the Aussie, and then he suddenly closed his eyes and reached his hand to his temple and said, "Just a minute . . . I'm getting a very strong picture of . . . of a camera."

"What?" the Australian fellow said.

"Just a minute . . . no, there are two cameras, and you are holding one, while a short woman—very beautiful—with brown hair is holding the other."

The fellow looked stunned. "That's my wife . . . we're both photographers. How did . . . how did. . . ?"

"Just a minute," Rob continued, now holding both hands to his temples. "I see one, two, three children . . . and the number 15. Does the number fifteen mean something to you?"

The man's eyes were big as golf balls. "Why, yes, yes . . . it's our fifteenth anniversary. I've . . . I've never experienced anything like. . . ." The poor chap, now almost incapable of breathing, asked, "Who are you? What are you?"

Rob now opened his eyes, and smiled his most sincere pastoral smile, "Why I'm a pastor," he said, "a servant of God."

The Australian's eyes grew even larger, and he said, "Well, I don't go to church myself, but I can tell you, our pastors in Australia don't do anything like that!"

At that, Rob added, "Actually, I met your wife in here about fifteen minutes ago. . . ."

Then the fellow put his hand to his forehead, closed his eyes, and doubled over laughing, as did Rob. For the next few minutes, to the amusement of all the other customers, the two of them were staggering around the carry-out, howling with laughter. Finally, the Australian fellow put his arm around Rob and said, "Our ministers down under don't do anything like *that* either!"

When I heard Rob's story, after laughing nearly to tears myself, I thought, *Rob's sense of humor may have said something even more wonderful about God than any supernatural insight would have.* It said about him exactly what Peter said about himself: I'm just a human being like you!

We have to remember that when God decided to go far beyond sending us verbal messages through the prophets, when God in some mysterious way "showed up" himself "in person" through Christ, God's presence was marvelously human as well as miraculous. Jesus slept, ate, sweat, tired, cried, and suffered like us all. God communicated his message, not *in spite of* Jesus' humanity, but *through it, because of it.* So Peter's words, "I am only a man myself" teach us apprentices something profound about spiritual friendship: Never be ashamed of your humanity!

As Peter's story continues, he does not proceed by preaching, but rather by conversing: "Talking *with* him"—not "to" or "at" him—Peter says to the assembled entourage, "You are well aware that it is against our law for a Jew to associate with a Gentile or visit him. But God has shown me that I should not call any man impure or unclean."

Do you feel how powerful this statement is? Peter is beginning by showing profound respect for the people of the "wrong" religion and ethnic origin. And instead of showing them how much they have to learn from him, he expresses what he is now learning through this experience with them. "God has shown me," he says, and in so doing, he in a sense qualifies himself as a "safe" spiritual teacher by first showing himself a humble learner.

When we become spiritual friends as Peter did with Cornelius, we similarly become sensitive to issues of language. We become uncomfortable labeling people. Whether it's "impure or unclean" or more contemporary labels like "unsaved," "non-Christian," "lost," or "pagan," we become increasingly sensitive to the way that such in-grouping and out-grouping can itself be sub-Christian behavior. On the one hand, by using such language we can un-intentionally elevate ourselves to a superior category; on the other hand, such language can degrade others—in our minds or to their ears or both. Either way, careless language sabotages spiritual friendship.

One of the more common terms used these days to label non-Christians by Christians—and in particular, by the Christians most oriented toward evangelism—is "lost people." The term comes from Jesus' stories of the lost sheep, lost coin, and lost son in Luke 15. Unfortunately, the term, which in the story means loved, precious, and sought after, can become on our lips a synonym for "impure" or "unclean." Do you feel the implied judgment of calling someone "lost"—especially as compared to calling them "missed" or "treasured," which might be better terms to describe the sheep, coin, and son in the stories? As a former English teacher, I may seem hypersensitive to language issues, but Peter gives us all good reason to make certain that our language is respectful. The concern for respect apparently stayed with him, considering again what he wrote years later: "Always be prepared to give an answer to everyone who asks you to give the reason for the hope that you have. But do this with gentleness and respect" (1 Peter 3:15).

Sometimes I wonder if we would be wiser to apply the term "lost" to ourselves. After all, if you send a letter to someone and it never arrives, you say the letter is lost. Similarly, God has sent us into the world as ambassadors and agents of God's love, and yet many of us have never really arrived at our destination. So, in that light, who is lost—them or us?

6 | Reaching Christians for Christ

Peter does not speak to Cornelius and friends from a position of superior privilege and power, but rather he comes to them somewhat off-balance, almost dazed by what is happening. Peter says, in essence, "Look, I'm outside my comfort zone just by being here. I'm taking a risk just to enter your home, just to be your friend. Being here violates my long-held religious standards ... so I'm learning right along with you." And then, before he proclaims anything to them, he pays them the added respect of listening: "May I ask why you sent for me?"

Even after hearing about Cornelius's vision, he still does not teach, but rather repeats again that he himself is learning through this experience: "I now realize how true it is that God does not show favoritism but accepts [people] from every nation who fear him and do what is right." And then, finally, he begins to teach, but even so, he emphasizes not their ignorance but how much they already know: "You know... You know..." he repeats. Finally, he gets to the core of his message: "We are witnesses of everything [Jesus] did in the country of the Jews and in Jerusalem. They killed him by hanging him on a tree, but God raised him from the dead on the third day and caused him to be seen. He was not seen by all the people, but by witnesses whom God had already chosen—by us who ate and drank with him after he rose from the dead. He commanded us to preach to the people and to testify that he is the one whom God appointed as judge of the living and the dead. All the prophets testify about him that everyone who believes in him receives forgiveness of sins through his name" (Acts 10:39–43).

And Peter can get no further. That is all Cornelius and the other people need to hear. They believe and God's Spirit fills them. Peter baptizes them—a radical act, since they are the first Gentiles to be so marked as disciples. But the story does not end there.

Before long, the Christians back in Judea hear what Peter has done, and they are critical—critical exactly as Jesus' critics, the Pharisees, had been critical of Jesus a few months earlier: "You went into the house of uncircumcised men and ate with them," they say. In other words, "You extended friendship to the 'wrong' people, to outsiders." (Do you feel the sad irony here, that Jesus' so-called followers have so quickly switched sides, playing the role of Pharisees—in just a matter of a few years? The irony is stunning, depressing, jolting—a stinging warning to all of us today.) In response, Peter tells the story of his spiritual friendship with Cornelius and company, concluding with this powerful statement and question: "The Holy Spirit came on them as he had come on us at the beginning. Then I remembered what the Lord had said: 'John baptized with water, but you will be baptized with the Holy Spirit.' So if God gave them the same gift as he gave us, who believed in the Lord Jesus Christ, who was I to think that I could oppose God?" (Acts 11:15–17).

His statement (actually a question—in light of what we have said earlier about questions, do you see why phrasing it as a question was such a good idea?) leads to one of the happier endings in the whole Bible: "When they heard this, they had no further objections and praised God, saying, 'So then, God has granted even the Gentiles repentance unto life.'"

Peter learns, the Christians back in Judea learn, just as Cornelius and his entourage have learned: Everybody is transformed through the process of spiritual friendship.

Just as Peter remembered some of Jesus' words when explaining the baptism of the Gentiles, right now I remember how Jesus said he would be with his followers and how his Spirit would teach them as they went into the world to make disciples. *Making disciples* is the more biblical term for *evangelism* and the original way of saying "engaging in spiritual friendship." I remember how Jesus said there were lessons he wanted to teach them but they could not yet bear to learn, and I wonder if this lesson was one of them: that the door of God's acceptance would be opened to all people, whatever their background, with no favoritism.

I also wonder if there are lessons that we can only learn as we, like Peter, leave our comfort zones, as our old categories are stretched beyond the breaking point, as we engage in spiritual friendship with the Corneliuses around us, as we become learners as we teach, as we refuse to place ourselves on a higher plane than anyone else, and as we show respect to those to whom we have been sent.

And I wonder if it conversely might be true that if we are not engaged in spiritual friendship in this radical way, there are things we can never learn as disciples—no matter how many Bible studies we join, classes and courses we complete, sermons we take notes on, verses we memorize, doctrines we affirm. Might spiritual friendship be an essential dimension of our own training as disciples, an experience we need as much as others do?

And further, might it be fair to say that we cannot really call ourselves disciples if we are not following Jesus' and Peter's example of being "friends of sinners"—spiritual friends who love, accept, learn with, and teach those who are missed by God, precious to God?

That is why I say that when spiritual friendship happens, when real evangelism happens, it is the Christians who are converted first.

My friend Skip Smith sometimes says that his ministry is "reaching Christians for Christ," and that is how I feel as I write this chapter. I feel that some Christian readers may be ready to be converted into a new kind of Christian—not Christians who judge, remain aloof, feel superior, disrespect those who do not believe—but rather Christians who join Jesus and Peter in befriending others, and believing that as they do, *everyone involved* will become closer to God, closer to Christ.

That is how it has been with Alice and me. She is not the only one growing through our friendship. I am learning and growing too. My conversion is ongoing, as is hers.

7 | There's No Conflict in My Mind

I must have responded to Alice's email by talking a bit more about my hypothesis—that many postmodern people are really seeking God and open to God, but they stumble at the modern "version" of God that is presented to them by too many Christians and churches:

- an uptight God who is about black-and-white easy answers and brittle, rigid logic and law, rather than about profound and many-faceted truth, self-sacrificing love, compassionate justice, and profound relationships
- a conceptual God who is encountered through systems of abstractions, propositions, and terminology rather than through an amazing story, intense poetry, beauty, experience, experiment, and community
- a controlling God who is cold, analytical, and mechanistic rather than a master artist and lover who is passionate about good and evil, justice and injustice, beauty and desecration, hope and cynicism
- an exclusive God who favors insiders and is biased against outsiders rather than a God of scandalous inclusion, amazing mercy, and shocking acceptance, who blesses "insiders" so they can extend the blessing to "outsiders," thus making everyone an insider

a tense God who prefers people to become judgmental, arrogant, and closed-minded rather than compassionate, humble, and teachable.

I must have suggested to Alice that the God of the Bible is far more wild and alive and "out of the box" than the modern version. I may have also said again that the best place to get an image of God is by looking at Jesus, not at the wordy, windy, systematic explanations of God too often given by preachers like me. And I may have further said that a postmodern version of Christianity will be as different from the modern version as the varying views of God described above. I don't remember exactly what I said, but these are the kinds of things I typically say in conversations with my postmodern friends. Anyway, here is how she responded:

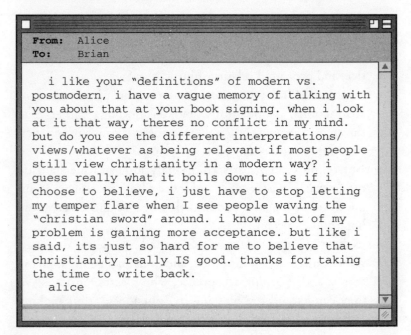

From: Alice
To: Brian

i like your "definitions" of modern vs. postmodern, i have a vague memory of talking with you about that at your book signing. when i look at it that way, theres no conflict in my mind. but do you see the different interpretations/ views/whatever as being relevant if most people still view christianity in a modern way? i guess really what it boils down to is if i choose to believe, i just have to stop letting my temper flare when I see people waving the "christian sword" around. i know a lot of my problem is gaining more acceptance. but like i said, its just so hard for me to believe that christianity really IS good. thanks for taking the time to write back.
   alice

I hoped that my previous response would have been helpful, but I was completely unprepared for "when i look at it that way theres no conflict in my mind." Do you feel the significance of that statement?

Nor was I prepared for the depth of her follow-up question: "but do you see the different interpretations/views/whatever as being relevant if most people still view christianity in a modern way?" Let me try to expand or amplify that question for you, because I think it is more significant than it may appear at first glance.

I think Alice is saying something like this: If nearly all Christians in the world today are brain-locked in a modern paradigm of Christianity, does it really matter that there might be a postmodern paradigm for Christianity? If I become a Christian, but nearly all current Christians and churches are modern in their worldview, then won't I be forced to conform to their modernity as well as their Christianity? And if that is the case, does it matter that a postmodern version of Christianity is *possible,* since the only *actual* and *available* version is thoroughly modern? And if I am forced to conform to the modern form of Christianity, then aren't all my fears legitimate—that by becoming a Christian I will regress into a worse kind of person than I am now—"closed-minded and bigoted and brainwashed and everything bad"?

I find it fascinating that Alice's concern at this point is not about the *truth* of Christianity, but rather about the *goodness* of it. Others of my friends are far more concerned with the truth questions: Did Jesus really exist? Did he really perform miracles? Did he really rise from the dead? But even for them, truth is not an abstract, isolated category; it is integrated with goodness and with beauty.

My friends Rafael and Maria began attending my church a few years ago. Neither of them were committed Christians when they began attending, and I wondered how they were progressing in their spiritual search. We arranged to have lunch together, and over some authentic El Salvadoran food, I asked them, "So how are you two doing with God? I've noticed you're in church nearly every week."

Maria spoke up first: "We love it. The only time we're not at church is when our daughters have tennis tournaments on Sunday mornings. Basically, Brian, I'd have to say I'm there with God now. I know I used to be a skeptic, but now it all makes sense. In fact, I can't believe that I *used to* believe that everything just happened by chance. I don't know when it happened, really; there haven't been any epiphanies or lightning bolts. But I just know that I'm with God now."

Rafael looked a little suspicious. "You are? Wow, you never told me that. Brian, I'm not sure she's as far along as she's making you think. But as for me, I'm not there yet. I am making progress though. Here's what I know: Whatever it is that you and the people at your church have, I'm convinced that it's *beautiful*. I'm just not sure if I believe it's *true* yet."

Taken together, I think Alice and Rafael and Maria have something important to tell us. A person's decision to become a Christian is not simply a question of being convinced rationally about the truth of Christianity, although truth is an indispensable element of the decision. No, there is an integration of truth, beauty, and goodness that must come together to give a person confidence to step from relative uncommitment into Christian commitment.

The "Christian sword"—Christianity as conquest, argument, win-lose fight—comes up again, and it makes sense that it does, because Alice is questioning if Christianity is *good* as well as beautiful and true, and the strident, pushy, sharp, damaging, coercive tone she has encountered too often strikes her as neither good, beautiful, nor true.

This is another reason why spiritual friendship is so important. Maybe a person can learn something about Christian truth-claims through a sermon or a book. But the beauty and goodness of the Christian faith can only be experienced and evaluated through a relationship with a real live Christian, called an *advocate* by Lewis Rambo (*Understanding Religious Conversion*, Yale University Press, 1993). Or, better still, a spiritual seeker can be welcomed into a network of relationships with many advocates in a dynamic and accepting Christian community. Robert Webber emphasizes this communal dimension of the "Journey to Jesus": "This is post-modern evangelism—process in a relational and communal atmosphere of embodied faith, an awakening of faith in a healthy community of believers" (*Journey to Jesus*, Abingdon, 2001, p. 70). As Alice's next email makes clear, that is exactly where she is being drawn.

8 | It Hasn't Been an Issue Yet, But It Will Be

A few weeks later, I received this short message from Alice.

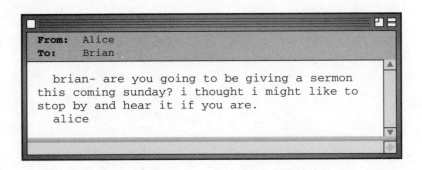

From: Alice
To: Brian

brian- are you going to be giving a sermon this coming sunday? i thought i might like to stop by and hear it if you are.
alice

As I recall, Alice did not make it that Sunday, and soon she returned home to Philadelphia for her summer break. But her interest in coming to church, though postponed, didn't disappear, as you will see in an upcoming email. Over the summer, we kept in touch. Her next contact with me made it clear that her spiritual search was not taking a summer break.

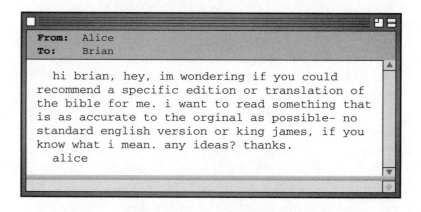

From: Alice
To: Brian

hi brian, hey, im wondering if you could
recommend a specific edition or translation of
the bible for me. i want to read something that
is as accurate to the orginal as possible- no
standard english version or king james, if you
know what i mean. any ideas? thanks.
alice

Of course, by "standard english" she means the "Elizabethan English" of "king james," and I did know what she meant. But as you will see in her next two messages, her difficulties with the Bible would not be solved by a contemporary translation.

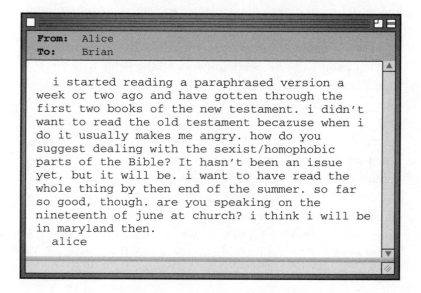

From: Alice
To: Brian

i started reading a paraphrased version a
week or two ago and have gotten through the
first two books of the new testament. i didn't
want to read the old testament becazuse when i
do it usually makes me angry. how do you
suggest dealing with the sexist/homophobic
parts of the Bible? It hasn't been an issue
yet, but it will be. i want to have read the
whole thing by then end of the summer. so far
so good, though. are you speaking on the
nineteenth of june at church? i think i will be
in maryland then.
alice

If you have grown up with the Bible, you have no idea how difficult the book can be for the uninitiated—until you enter a spiritual friendship with someone like Alice. Meanwhile, we preachers constantly reassure people that the Bible is simple and easy to understand, I suppose motivated by a desire to encourage people to read it. But our reassurances are counterproductive as well as dishonest. We would be better off preparing people realistically: The Bible is an extremely difficult book for modern and postmodern readers alike. (The Bible is more honest about itself in this regard than we are. See 2 Peter 3:15–16, for example.) It is definitely worth the effort, but make no mistake, it will take much effort.

At best, we are asking people to interact with texts and stories collected and written in diverse cultures, by diverse people, over a period of over two thousand years. We are asking them to be able to step out of their own modern and postmodern paradigms and into the worldviews of people far removed geographically and historically.

At worst (and I fear this is too often the case), we are expecting that people can properly understand the Bible by reading it through their modern and postmodern lenses, with little or no awareness of the cultural, political, social, geographical, economic, and philosophical realities in which the biblical documents emerged. And furthermore, we are expecting that they can do so independently, without the benefit of the Christian community—including its scholars, teachers, mystics, and mentors.

I remember the first time I began to realize how difficult the Bible can be for spiritual seekers. I was speaking to a group of visiting scholars from mainland China, all of whom had been reared under Maoist philosophy. In their experience, they informed me, religious people were old, uneducated, and female, so to have a relatively young educated male talk to them about faith in God was most intriguing. One fellow told me that he had begun reading what he called "the book Bible." "I think this is very bad for me," he said. "I think this book Bible makes me go away from believing in the God."

"Why?" I asked.

He replied, "Because I read about how the God tell the Jewish people they must kill all non-Jewish people around them, even the mothers and little children. I think to myself, if my ancestors are so unlucky and they live near Jewish people, the God would say kill them too. And then I would not exist. So, the book Bible makes me feel this God is not for me or my people."

What would you say to a comment like that? At the very least, you would have to sympathize with him—you can see his point. Of course, I as a descendent of ancient Celts am no more Jewish than my Chinese friend, but because I have been raised with the Bible, I instinctively (and perhaps inappropriately?) identify with the Jewish people, Gentile though I am. (If you gave him a pat modern-style "answer"—such as that Christians now are "heirs of the promise" of the Jewish people and therefore part of the "people of God"—that would not help with his legitimate historical question: How can I feel safe around a God who would have commanded the annihilation of my ancestors?)

These days, people are concerned about God's attitude toward contemporary women, minorities, and homosexuals—along with ancient Canaanites. Alice and postmodern people like her will need some fresh thinking from us about these concerns. As it turned out, Alice asked me for some fresh thinking in her next message.

9 | I Must Be Interpreting It Wrong, Right? (Or, Why Am I Even Trying to Like This?)

A few weeks passed before Alice sent me the following message:

From: Alice
To: Brian

Brian,
I was reading in Luke 12 and I got to the part where Jesus says he hasn't come in peace, but he came to pit brother against brother, and so on. Also, I'm confused as to why he told people that it was wrong for them to say goodbye to their families or bury their fathersbefore they followed him throughout the land. I don't mean to bombard you with questions, but if you get a moment, could you give me some insight into this? It really confused me. i thought jesus was supposed to bring peace, and i thought families were an important issue in christianity (at least, i know they are to the christian coalition). it doesn't make sense to me. i must be interpretting it wrong, right? just if you get a moment. . . thanks.
Alice

Fortunately, I do remember my basic response to these questions. As for the coming "to pit brother against brother," I created a scenario for her. Imagine, I said, that it is the 1960s and a young white teenager in the deep South, let's say the son of a prominent minister of an exclusively white church, becomes a committed follower of Christ. He begins to read the New Testament, and he becomes convinced that white Christians should love and accept their "Negro" brothers and sisters. He articulates this new belief to his father, his mother, and his siblings. Immediately a division occurs. Imagine that he then brings this issue up to the whole church. Or imagine that it is the late 1990s, and it is a young Serb who becomes a Christian and says that Serbs should love Croats and Kosovars. Or imagine … Alice got the point. In this way, by being an agent of peace and reconciliation, Jesus inevitably becomes (as his followers will also become) a cause for division and conflict. Jesus and his followers threaten the status quo—its biases, prejudices, and priorities.

As for the several passages where Jesus forbids potential disciples from burying or saying goodbye to their parents, which seems to undermine "family values," I offer two insights. First, in some cases, burying one's father may have been closely linked with getting one's inheritance. In other words, if someone says, "I will follow you, but let me gain financial security first through my inheritance," Jesus would respond, "No way. Pursuing God's kingdom isn't a hobby you pursue at the periphery of life. It has to be your central passion, your deepest desire. You can't serve God and money." Or if someone says, "I want to follow you, but I want to fit my commitment to you conveniently in around the edges of my primary family commitments," Jesus would say, "I'm sorry, but that's not the kind of commitment I'm looking for. The kingdom I am here to proclaim is a revolutionary matter calling for extraordinary commitment. It can't be conveniently accommodated in a status quo life."

These responses apparently helped Alice.

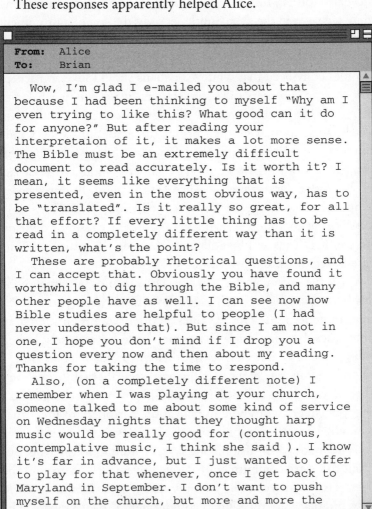

From: Alice
To: Brian

Wow, I'm glad I e-mailed you about that because I had been thinking to myself "Why am I even trying to like this? What good can it do for anyone?" But after reading your interpretaion of it, it makes a lot more sense. The Bible must be an extremely difficult document to read accurately. Is it worth it? I mean, it seems like everything that is presented, even in the most obvious way, has to be "translated". Is it really so great, for all that effort? If every little thing has to be read in a completely different way than it is written, what's the point?

These are probably rhetorical questions, and I can accept that. Obviously you have found it worthwhile to dig through the Bible, and many other people have as well. I can see now how Bible studies are helpful to people (I had never understood that). But since I am not in one, I hope you don't mind if I drop you a question every now and then about my reading. Thanks for taking the time to respond.

Also, (on a completely different note) I remember when I was playing at your church, someone talked to me about some kind of service on Wednesday nights that they thought harp music would be really good for (continuous, contemplative music, I think she said). I know it's far in advance, but I just wanted to offer to play for that whenever, once I get back to Maryland in September. I don't want to push myself on the church, but more and more the

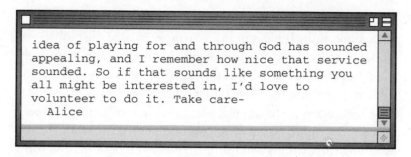

idea of playing for and through God has sounded
appealing, and I remember how nice that service
sounded. So if that sounds like something you
all might be interested in, I'd love to
volunteer to do it. Take care-
    Alice

Alice makes, understandably in my opinion, a double over-statement here—"every little thing has to be read in a completely different way than it is written." I would qualify "every little thing" and "completely different way," but again, I am sympathetic to how difficult the Bible can be for a person unfamiliar with it.

But then again, if we reframe the situation (remember how important the framing of an issue is?), I think we will become more impressed with how accessible and relevant the Bible is. Frame it like this: In spite of the fact that the Bible was written long ago and far away by many different writers in many different cultures, arising among people whose lives were radically different from our own, it still yields wisdom and insight and challenge and perspective to people today, so that we can find it abundantly "worthwhile to dig through the Bible."

I suppose here, as in many places in life, our problem is one of expectations. We are used to people writing for *us.* Newspapers and popular magazines pitch at an eighth grade reading level, easy for *all of us.* Textbooks are generally written not only by knowledgeable people, but by skilled educators who pay attention to *our* learning styles, attention spans, and format preferences. Popular novels (the ones most of us read, if we read them at all) are written to be popular, and that means easy for *us,* accessible to *us.* We assume, if the Bible is in any way inspired, that the Holy Spirit would be so kind and considerate as to similarly gear it exclusively to *us.* Reasonable enough ... at first glance. But think again. If the Bible were written for twenty-first century readers, how would it have come across to its original hearers, or hearers in the sixth century B.C., or eighth century A.D., or fourteenth century A.D.? And, assuming the world is still spinning, how would a style and form targeted on a primitive twenty-first century demographic cohort feel for advanced readers in the twenty-ninth century?

It is hard for us, spoiled as we are by being marketing targets, but the Bible asks us to rise above our narrow parochial tastes. It asks us to learn, to understand, to imaginatively enter an alien geography (Jerusalem, Nineveh, Bethany, Bethlehem), alien economies (denarii, talents, shekels), alien cultures, and social structures (polygamy, patriarchy, monarchy, tribal confederation, slavery, arranged marriages). It asks us to stop absolutizing our perspective and, instead, to see our modern or postmodern viewpoints simply as views from a point—limited, contingent, changing, not privileged. In so doing, the very form of the Bible begins teaching us something about humility and perspective.

10 | Well, Neither Did Jesus

But the Bible does not expect us (so to speak) to figure everything out alone. It assumes that there is a community that passes down the art of biblical literacy from generation to generation. If we resent the complexity of learning required to understand and live with the Bible, then we are showing our ignorance. Do Mozart, the Beatles, Dave Brubeck, Tupac Shakur, Madonna, or Britney Spears automatically "make sense" to anyone who is not part of the community of western music, and the respective subcommunities, like classical, oldies, jazz, rap, or pop communities? Of course not. These artists only "work" for you if you learn the musical traditions—the genres—in which they arise. If you doubt that, go to a music store and buy some Arabic music, or Chinese music, or even Renaissance music—and see how much sense it makes to you, and realize that for its primary audience, those "odd" sounds are beautiful. (Or conversely, imagine playing cool jazz or rap or heavy metal or baroque music to a tribesman in the jungle. Do you think he would instantly "get it" as you do?)

To understand anything, we need to apprentice ourselves to the community that honors what it is we want to understand. Thankfully, Alice is learning this without me telling her. Isn't it fascinating that after she says, "I can see now how Bible studies are helpful to people," she adds, "I had never understood that"? For the present time, I was a primary representative of the biblical community helping Alice understand the biblical message, but that would soon change.

Alice was concerned that the Bible needed to be read in a "completely different" way than it was written, but I think what the biblical community can help us do is exactly the reverse: To understand the Bible more as its original hearers would have understood it. (I say *hearers* because one of the other great differences between antiquity and now is our literacy—a historical oddity, the norm being that most people through history would have encountered the Bible by hearing it, not reading it themselves.) In other words, the biblical community does not aim to twist the Bible to fit our tastes and perspectives. Rather, it helps us adjust our frame of reference to try to reenter the biblical world and hear its message on the terms of its original hearers. First we let ourselves be absorbed into or abducted by the alien biblical world, and then we are able to let its message enter us, and then we bring that message back into our world.

As you would expect, sometimes the biblical community preserves its own biases. For example, a denomination that began in the sixteenth century might hallow the sixteenth-century worldview without realizing it—and thus its biblical interpretations would be just as limited as a twenty-first century reader's would. This is one reason why biblical communities need scholars who scrutinize our interpretations with an accumulating store of historical insight; however, we need more than scholars. We need people like Alice who come among us and ask questions we have never asked before, satisfied as we are with the interpretations of our communities. Do you see this? Do you see how the community is enriched by Alice with her questions just as she is enriched by the community and its answers?

The story of another spiritual friendship illustrates this beautifully. I remember the day George came into my office. I had seen him at church over the last several months, but never really talked to him. He looked nervous—*real* nervous. "I've really been dreading this appointment," he said.

"I hope I'm not that intimidating, George," I said. "What's going on?"

He said, "It's just that I've really enjoyed coming to Cedar Ridge for the last few months. You have no idea how much this church has helped me. I can't explain it, but I find myself crying nearly every service. Anyway, that's why I've dreaded this meeting. I'm afraid that after today, I won't be welcome there."

I wasn't sure what could be so terrible that he would no longer be welcome. I said, "Well, before we get into that, tell me about your spiritual journey up to this point."

He explained that until a few months earlier, he had been an atheist. After a messy divorce, he had begun seeing a counselor. After several private sessions, the counselor recommended group therapy for George. The first few sessions, George just listened. Then, one night, it was his turn to open up. "I told them everything. You see, Brian, my marriage fell apart because I was unfaithful, not just once but many times. I am terribly ashamed of that part of my life. I began to cry, and when I finished telling them everything, they just gathered around me and hugged me. And I can't explain it, but at that moment, when I was accepted in spite of all the crap that I had done, I knew there was a God."

"That's what brought me to Cedar Ridge," he said. "I wanted to get stronger in my relationship with God. And the church has helped so much."

"Well, what's the problem, then, George? It sounds like you're really making progress," I said.

"Well, it's this: Even though I've been coming to Cedar Ridge for all this time, I am still no closer to believing in Jesus Christ. I believe in God now, but Jesus just doesn't make sense to me," he said.

"What about Jesus doesn't make sense?" I asked.

"It's not his teachings. I find them powerful and beautiful and challenging. It's the part about him having to die on the cross. I guess if there's one question I'd have for you, it would be this: *Why did Jesus have to die?*"

Instantly, two thoughts hit me. First, I realized that the way he was asking the question was a way I had never before asked or had been asked it. Second, I realized that none of my answers fit the way he was asking it. He was not asking for an answer *within* the framework of Christian theology, so talking about Christ's death as a substitutionary or atoning sacrifice would not help him—that kind of explanation was exactly, I guessed, what did not make sense to him.

What he was asking, I guessed (and then confirmed by asking him for clarification), was this: If God was going to forgive us, why didn't he just forgive us? Why did Jesus have to die so that we could be forgiven? Having an innocent person die for guilty people did not seem to solve the "injustice" of forgiveness—it only seemed to add to the injustice. So, why did Jesus have to die?

"George," I said, "you're asking this question in a more profound way than I think I'm prepared to answer it. So I wonder ... would you give me two weeks to think about this? Could we get together again in two weeks?" He said sure, and immediately after he left, I pulled some of my theological texts down off my shelves—John Stott, J. I. Packer, James Boice, and others—but they all said exactly the kinds of things I would have said to George. They answered a lot of important questions, but not this one.

I continued to pray, think, reflect, and study over the next two weeks, trying to answer George's question, but the deadline was looming and I really had nothing new to offer. A day or two before our appointment, I was relaxing in my parents' swimming pool with my brother, Peter. Now Peter is a mechanical engineer. He is a bright, sincere, and committed Christian, but not an obvious candidate to help me with my theological mystery. I asked him how the engineering business was going, and he reciprocated: "How's the ministry world going?"

"Okay," I said, "except that a couple weeks ago I realized that I don't know why Jesus had to die."

Then Peter, without skipping a beat, without even a moment's hesitation, said, "Well, neither did Jesus."

"What?" I said, making a kind of strange face.

Then Peter said, "Remember the story about Jesus in the Garden of Gethsemane? He was praying that if there were any other way for him to accomplish his mission, he hoped God would spare him from dying. But then he said 'Not my will, but your will be done.' So it sounds to me like Jesus didn't really understand why it had to be that way either. But the point wasn't understanding it; the point was doing what needed to be done."

I shook my head and said, "Wow, I never thought of it that way before," and I wondered why Stott, Packer, Boice, and the others hadn't ever mentioned Peter's answer. I had no other great insights, so when George and I met a day or two later, I simply recounted the story of Jesus in the Garden of Gethsemane, just as Peter had told it to me in the pool. I'll never forget George's response.

"Hmmm. Hmmm. Wow. You know ... for some reason ... that doesn't answer my question, but somehow, that's better than an

answer. It kind of makes the question not really matter so much."
And it was as if a barrier had been removed. Over the next few
weeks, George progressed in his faith to the point of becoming a
committed follower of Jesus.

Two things strike me from this episode with George. First, I
am struck by the power of the story itself. Peter didn't offer me
some abstract angle on George's question; he brought me back to
the simple facts of the story, and the story itself helped George
more than any abstractions could have. Second, I am struck by
the dynamic way George—a newcomer to the community of
faith—challenged me in my understanding, pushing me to consult the community (through books in my library, and through
Pete in my parents' pool), leading to a new insight—something
that I bring back to the community, thus enriching what it has to
offer the next person who comes along. To say that the best theologians I had ever read never got me thinking as George did is
not to insult the theologians, but rather to affirm the value of
people like George and Alice to the Christian community. As with
Peter and Cornelius, the relationship isn't one-way. As is true in
all good friendships, the benefit is mutual—it flows both ways . . .
as in a dance.

11 | The Idea of Playing for and through God

Let's go back to the last part of the previous message from Alice.

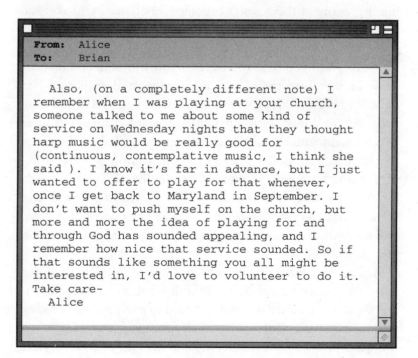

```
From:   Alice
To:     Brian

   Also, (on a completely different note) I
remember when I was playing at your church,
someone talked to me about some kind of
service on Wednesday nights that they thought
harp music would be really good for
(continuous, contemplative music, I think she
said ). I know it's far in advance, but I just
wanted to offer to play for that whenever,
once I get back to Maryland in September. I
don't want to push myself on the church, but
more and more the idea of playing for and
through God has sounded appealing, and I
remember how nice that service sounded. So if
that sounds like something you all might be
interested in, I'd love to volunteer to do it.
Take care-
   Alice
```

The service Alice referred to was actually on Thursday nights. It is now called *Intermission* (a break during your week), but back then it was called *Anam* (a Celtic word for soul, suggesting "time for your soul"). It is an unusual, experimental kind of service, focusing on contemplative prayer. It flows from a hunch that we have, that people don't just want to learn about spiritual disciplines and be told to practice them on their own; they want and need the chance to actually practice them together.

I am fortunate that the church I am privileged to serve understands something that too few churches understand: *Sometimes belonging must precede believing*. In other words, unless we let not-yet-Christians enter and participate in the Christian community, many of them won't become Christians. Perhaps this is so obvious that you wonder how anyone could doubt it. But sadly, that understanding is still pretty rare. If you wonder why, I have to point you back to history. Many of our denominations arose or redefined themselves during the modern period (say between 1500 and 2000), when theological controversy and competition, combined with a penchant toward control (all in an environment where modern Christianity provided the dominant worldview), reinforced what I call "motivation by exclusion." Motivation by exclusion says something like this: *We're on the inside, but you're on the outside. We're right, and you're wrong. If you want to come inside, then you need to be right. So, just believe right, think right, speak right, and act right, and we'll let you in.*

Again, there were reasons why this line of thinking predominated in modern churches, but I think for those of us living and serving in a postmodern world, we need to move beyond motivation by exclusion. Our motivation by acceptance will say something like this: *We are a community bound together and energized by faith, love, and commitment to Jesus Christ. Even though you don't yet share that faith, love, and commitment, you are most welcome to be with us, to belong here, to experience what we're about. Then, if you are attracted and persuaded by what you see, you'll want to set down roots here long-term. And even if you don't, you'll always be a friend.*

This approach is more in sync with Jesus' own example. He was criticized for being a "friend of sinners"—in other words, he welcomed and accepted people who did not yet "believe right, think right, speak right, and act right." But he knew something we need to know: If people can belong long enough to observe how God is alive among us, if people can belong long enough to see authentic love among us, if they can belong long enough to see whatever good exists in our lives as individuals and as a community, they can come to believe.

So, I told the leaders of Anam about Alice, and they welcomed her in, and her harp playing was beautiful. It enriched the Anam community immeasurably, and she became well loved. Nobody asked "Is she a believer yet?" They just accepted her.

Don't you love that phrase, "playing for and through God"? Accepting Alice meant accepting her talents, and letting her give as well as receive. We have seen the same thing happen again and again. Two other stories further reflect this acceptance.

Chai is an Asian woman who was invited to Cedar Ridge by a friend. She was Buddhist by birth, but (like many nominal Christians) knew next to nothing of her religion's devotion, teaching, or practice. She heard that our acting group was looking for members, and she had been active in community theatre so she went to an audition and was accepted. The vast majority of Cedar Ridge people assumed that Chai was a Christian. I know that when word got out that she was not, a few people were concerned.

One Sunday we wanted to highlight this idea of belonging before believing, so before the sermon, we asked Chai to share her story. She came up to the microphone and said, "I was brought up as a Buddhist, so I never knew anything about Christianity before coming here. And actually, I still do not call myself a Christian, although I am learning a lot about God and faith. I am so grateful that I have been accepted here, because otherwise, how would I learn what Christianity is all about?"

It was a moving moment. I remember that after the service, a woman came up to me and said, "If I had heard about Chai without hearing her speak herself, I would have been against her being 'on stage' in the acting group since she's not a Christian. But after hearing her, how can I object?"

As far as I know, Chai has still not come to Christian commitment, but I am glad that we have been able to give her "a safe place to hear a dangerous message," as Bill Hybels says.

Like Chai, Mike belonged for so long that people assumed he believed. (When I say "belonged," I don't mean that he was an official member; I mean that he was accepted into the community without reservation.) I first met Mike one summer when a group of us from church played volleyball every Wednesday evening at a local park. One evening as we were playing, I noticed a guy walking through the park, looking over in our direction. I felt a little nudge from the Holy Spirit, so I momentarily dropped out of the game, ran across a field to where he was walking, and said, "Hey, would you like to play?" He said sure and joined in. After the game, I said, "You're welcome to come back next week. We play every Wednesday." He said, "Are you guys in some sort of league or something?" I said, "No, we all go to the same church." (I didn't want to say "I'm the pastor"—that can ruin a conversation pretty quick.) He asked about the church, and I told him he was welcome to check it out. He began attending soon, as I recall.

Mike was an agnostic; he was not especially close to Christian commitment. I think it was nearly two years before he began to believe. I remember asking him what finally brought him into faith, and this is what he told me: "I think that after six or eight months, a lot of the other singles about my age just sort of assumed I was a Christian. So they began telling me all of their problems and asking me to pray for them. I didn't have the nerve to tell them I didn't believe in prayer, but I would listen anyway. Something really funny happened. When they started telling me all of their problems, I realized that they were as messed up as I was! And somehow, when I realized they could be Christians and still have problems, I realized I could be a Christian too."

Belonging precedes believing for more and more people like Alice, Chai, and Mike. They need to see Christians living out their faith. They need an entrée into the Christian community.

If you agree with this, watch out because it will complicate your life—at least, your church life. As soon as you start inviting your spiritual friends into your church, you will begin to notice all of the unintentional Not Welcome signs posted around your church. Let me briefly mention four common ones.

1. **The Insider Language sign.** Do you know what the words *righteousness, Zion, sin, hell, circumcision, lost, saved, the Fall, great commission,* and *pagan* mean to your non-Christian friends? Do they have the same meanings as they do for those in your church?

2. **The Politically Correct sign.** Is it okay for someone to be politically liberal (or conservative) or Democrat (or Republican) or pro-choice (or pro-life) and attend your church, or

will they be insulted regularly and passionately as "them," not "us"?

3. **The Married Only sign.** What if your friend is single, gay, divorced, or living with someone outside of marriage? Will he or she be made to feel inferior or condemned or hated at your church?

4. **The Unusual Tolerances sign.** Everybody at your church knows that Sister Margaret can't sing, but everybody lets her do a solo every other month or so because ... well, just because she would be really brokenhearted to find out we all do not love her singing as much as she does. And everybody knows that the bathrooms smell really bad, and that the interior design is pathetic, and that old Ben is a little crazy and stares at people in odd ways. But the insiders have learned to tolerate these things ... which makes the outsiders feel odd. ("Do these people not notice, or do they really think this woman can sing?")

I know, you will have a list of "yes, but's" to counter this list. I won't try to answer your "yes, but's." I don't have any easy solutions. (It is no easy task to show acceptance for Sister Margaret without showing rejection for people with, uh, normal musical tastes!) I told you this concern would complicate your life!

But this is a *good* reason to complicate your life. In fact, if your church requires people to believe before belonging—if they have to believe right, think right, speak right, and act right before they will be accepted into your community—then I believe that either you will drive yourself, your church, or your spiritual friends crazy; or you will try to change your church, change churches, or give up the kind of spiritual friendship we are talking about, settling back into comfortable religious friendships with "believe-right, think-right, speak-right, act-right" people. And if you do *that,* frankly, I think you are doing the *wrong* thing because Jesus was not like that. In fact, Jesus was hated and rejected by people like that. But that is another story.

Let's return to Alice. Even though she began playing almost every week at Anam, I seldom saw her because my travel schedule kept me away most Thursday nights. In fact, since our original meeting, I only had seen her in person two or three times— once or twice at Anam and once at her fall recital. I was glad my travel schedule allowed me to attend her recital with my family because it was a way of demonstrating that I really was a spiritual friend (not just a pastor-guy trying to help someone as a "project"), and because the music was wonderful.

By the way, to be spiritual friends in this way, I think we will find ourselves attending a lot more recitals, soccer games, movies, festivals, parties, and concerts, which will mean we might have to cut back on some of our church activities. But then again (don't tell your pastor I said this, okay?), I think a lot of us would become a lot better Christians if we spent less time at church.

I know that was true for me. I remember back in the late 1980s, shortly after I had left my career in higher education to work in the church. After a year or so, I realized that I had lost all my non-Christian friends. My whole life was wrapped up with church people. Deep down, one of my primary spiritual gifts is evangelism, so I was deeply unsatisfied with my ecclesiastical isolation. So, over the next few years I changed my lifestyle. First, I began coaching my kids' soccer teams, something I enjoyed and had some talent for, and something that put me back in touch with non-church people (several of whom have since become followers of Christ, thanks be to God). Then I began pursuing a hobby of mine—wildlife and the outdoors—by volunteering to do wildlife surveys for the department of natural resources in my state. Through this volunteer work, I had a lot of fun (and still do), and met many people who have become and remained friends, with whom I have had many productive spiritual conversations. Some of them have also become followers of Christ. In general, I decided that all things being equal, if I had the chance to spend time with an non-church person and a church person, I would get together with the non-church person first, because the odds were, I'd find it much easier to connect with the church person later.

I suppose you could sum up this change in thinking like this: I decided to be a neighbor again, something I had become "too religious" for in the previous few years. If we take Jesus' teachings to heart, neighboring is a pretty essential spiritual practice. But too many of us Christians are invisible, absent neighbors, no neighbors at all—always running to church, to Bible study, to committee meetings, never having time to play golf or go for a walk or catch a cup of coffee with a neighbor (or help a mugged Samaritan lying beside the highway). Sadly, I don't think there will be a nationwide Christian radio broadcast called "Focus on the Neighborhood" anytime soon. But there should.

One of my proudest moments as a pastor came when I got a call from a woman who introduced herself like this: "You don't know me. I don't attend church." Then she continued, "But if I ever do attend church, it will be your church." She had my attention!

"Why do you say that?" I asked.

"It's because of the Jacksons," she said. "Before they moved down the street from me, I lived in a housing development. Now I live in a neighborhood. They are like the soul of this community. They're always having parties and inviting everyone over. They're always there if someone needs to talk. I just wanted you to know that if your church teaches people to be like the Jacksons, it must be a good church."

Another couple in my church, Jay and Kim, comes to mind. To tell you the truth, their Sunday attendance is not all that great, but that is because they have become the "chaplains" of their neighborhood. A few years ago, a child in the neighborhood was tragically killed. Jay and Kim sprang into action. Within hours, meals were being arranged for the bereaved family. A neighborhood prayer meeting was called, and neighbors who probably had little experience or belief in prayer gathered because they wanted to do something . . . anything . . . to help their neighbors. The whole neighborhood got a taste of true spirituality that night. The neighborhood has never been the same. Just the other night, Jay called me (he has done this several times) to get some pastorly advice about helping some folks in his neighborhood. He is a dentist by profession and Kim is an architect, but in their neighborhood, they are the pastors. They are true evangelists.

It is people like the Jacksons and Jay and Kim that make me love the benediction most of all each Sunday. At the benediction, I raise my hand and send everyone out to serve and love God and their neighbors. I send people out to do what the Jacksons and Jay and Kim have done so well—to hear the music, live the dance, and help others learn to dance too.

If this were a service at my church and you were present, I would offer you this benediction to send you on your way: "May the Spirit of Christ empower you to love and serve your neighbors, welcoming them into your lives and homes and schedules and hearts, so that through belonging they may discover the joys of believing and becoming. You are more ready for this than you realize. Go in God's grace and peace!"

12 | On the Verge of Tears . . . Since I Woke Up

I asked Alice if she would play at our Sunday Celebrations on the last Sunday morning of October. It was a special "Friends Day," and I thought that harp music would add a special touch (which it did). As far as I can remember, that was the first time she had ever come on a Sunday—and she got a double treatment, since she played at both 9:00 and 11:00 A.M. I checked my email late that night and found this message waiting:

From: Alice
To: Brian

hi brian,
I just got up from a _three and a half_ hour nap (taken immediately afteri returned home from church). i was thinking about emailing you before i fell asleep becuase i wanted to tell you how much i enjoyed your message today. you are such a wonderful speaker, but on top of that, WHAT YOU SAY is just so incredible- and im not just talking about this sunday. ill never forget the things you said at the first anam i attended. You were speaking about how everything in life has meaning. it was incredible. im sure you know this already, but you have such a wonderful gift.
i had a dream during my nap that i wanted to

---

tell you about. Im not one to get really
excited by dreams or anything like that, and i
feel sort of weird telling you, but i just have
to. im not really sure of all the circumstances
surrounding the dream, like why exactly you and
i were alone together talking about god and
music, but we were. so for a long time, thats
all the dream was. my parents walked in and you
met my parents, and my grandfather (who is
dead, has been for awhile) walked through as
well. for some reason, out of the blue (though
in the dream, it didnt feel like it was out of
the blue) you poured FREEZING cold water on my
head and said the baptism thing ("in the name
of the father, the son," etc, etc). it was
dripping all down my face, everywhere. . . so
much water, and it felt so good, and i just
started to cry and saying over again "thank
you. thank you so much." i said to you "i have
been thinking about this for awhile, but wasn't
sure i was ready", and you said "youve been
ready for a long time" and gave me a hug.

then i guess there was sort of a dream segue
type thing, and i was sitting with my friend
kate, who at the last minute cancelled out of
going to my recital. i was sitting with her
giving her the cold shoulder because she had
missed it and it hurt my feelings. then i
remembered: wait a second, theres no turning back
now, jesus wouldnt have done this, and you have
no right to. and i just apologized to kate and
siad "its okay. . . it went well and i understand
why you couldnt make it, and of course our
friendship is just as strong as always."

then i woke up. i dont know. . . it just
really affected me, ive felt like ive been on
the verge of tears (happy tears) since i woke
up. thank you for helping me bring about such a
change in my life.
   Alice

Now I find these words moving—in fact, reading them just now choked me up a couple of times. But before we get to the main issues of this email, let's deal with a peripheral issue.

When Alice recalls a talk I gave at our contemplative service about how "everything in life has meaning," she is referring to a brief talk I gave on what Christians would call "the doctrine of creation." It is significant that this talk impressed her so profoundly, because one of the streams of Christian belief that nearly disappeared during the spiritual drought of modernity was creation. Sadly, over the last few centuries, creation became "nature," and as such became the domain of physics, chemistry, astronomy, and biology. When Christians tried to talk about creation, it was usually in an ill-conceived (in fact, I would say disastrous) debate over evolution, one of our many tragic adventures in missing the point.

So, in the talk—it was more like a brief meditation really—at Anam, I simply tried to help people imagine what it would be like to live in a world that really was God's creation. In such a world, I suggested, there is nothing purely "objective"—meaning there is nothing that does not have a personal value attached to it. Why? Because if God is Creator, and God has feelings for everything God has made, then every atom in the universe is not a neutral objective object; rather, it is the artwork—beloved artwork—of a Creator who values every square centimeter of space, every moment in time, every quark, muon, gluon, neutrino, and proton; every whale, sparrow, chipmunk, and child. In other words, as we wander through the universe, we are not just encountering meaningless stuff; rather, we are walking through an art gallery, filled with objects full of meaning, expressiveness, revelation of the Creator's heart, intelligence, compassion, and whimsy. In addition, we are never walking through bland "public property" that "nobody owns," but rather we are always on God's private property, and everything we encounter belongs to God and matters to God. "This is my Father's world," as the old hymn says. It has a huge subjective value placed upon it, whether we value it or not, because God, the Supreme Subject, values it.

This view of things, I suggested, would result in a different attitude toward every part of life—toward ecology and endangered species, toward manufacturing (is this a good use of God's precious elements?), toward architecture (would this design do honor to the precious space that God has created?), toward leisure and work and recreation (are we dishonoring God's gift of time through workaholism or laziness or half-heartedness or boredom?), and certainly toward our treatment of one another. After asking everyone to imagine such a world, I suggested that this is the world that actually exists. This is basically all I said. I simply stated that in the beginning, God created the heavens and the earth, and that fact means that everything has meaning.

That this made such an impact on Alice tells us something amazing and exciting: In our postmodern world, the simple elements of our Christian belief mosaic are unspeakably precious and profound again. They aren't "oh, yes, of course..."—but rather, "it was incredible ... I'll never forget it." This wonderful new situation, where the simple and basic elements of our faith suddenly become magical and valuable again, explains why I find theological quibbling over theological esoterica in such bad taste and such a sad, if not downright wicked, waste of time. The beauty of "in the beginning God created" should make us giddy with joy and speechless with wonder for decades, leaving us little time to argue over ... over stuff I don't even want to dignify by mentioning here. Do you see what I mean? Maybe if we lived to be 750 years old, we could get so used to the wonder of the simple and basic elements of our faith that we could move on to some of these finer points ... but then again, I suspect that a person who had grown wiser and wiser for 750 years would be even more blown away by the simple truths like "in the beginning God..."

In this light, it is worth noting that Alice's kind words about my speaking are overshadowed, just as they should be, by her words "WHAT YOU SAY is just so incredible." Maybe you will agree with me that much of our preaching feels pumped up, inflated, like a sales pitch, as if we are trying to make mediocre news sound really, really good. And that is because too much of the time we are preaching points of our belief system that are only peripherally related to the heart of the real and ultimate good news. If we would rediscover the substance, the essence, the heart of our good news, we would have to work less on *how* we say what we say because *what* we say would in itself be so powerful.

Now, to the heart of Alice's message to me. What happened here? Was the dream reported in the previous chapter a bona fide spiritual experience, or was it just a psychological event? Or is that question itself (remember what we said about framing questions?) so poorly framed as to deserve not an answer, but a critique of the question (especially the word *just*)? Wouldn't you agree that any spiritual experience, if it passes through the psyche (and how could it not, if it is an experience?), would be psychological as well as spiritual? So maybe this is not the real question. Maybe the real question is, "Is this dream from God, or just from Alice's psyche? Is it a supernatural dream, or just a natural one?" And again, I wonder, is that a useful question, and what does the word *just* tell us about our presuppositions in framing the question? How sure are we that terms like "natural" and "supernatural" aren't in themselves confusions, red herrings, distortions, impositions from modernity that we should drop in favor of seeing the whole world as natural/supernatural, or, better put, wonderful? Would a dream like this that came purely ("just") from Alice's psyche (meaning from her imagination, her own inner processing of her spiritual journey so far) be of less value because it arose from within her? Or isn't that the point—that a dream like this is telling us what is happening in Alice's psyche? In other words, if God is in some way becoming real to Alice, isn't this exactly the kind of dream we might expect?

By suggesting that her dream is in a sense expected, I don't want to minimize the surprise of it because it really has a splendid uniqueness, doesn't it? Every detail rings with meaning (as we would expect in God's world!). Here it is again:

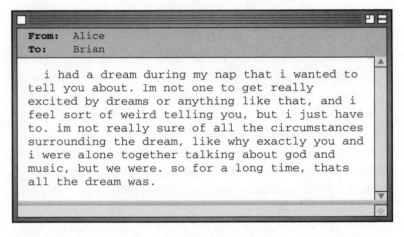

From: Alice
To: Brian

   i had a dream during my nap that i wanted to tell you about. Im not one to get really excited by dreams or anything like that, and i feel sort of weird telling you, but i just have to. im not really sure of all the circumstances surrounding the dream, like why exactly you and i were alone together talking about god and music, but we were. so for a long time, thats all the dream was.

In the dream, we are talking about God and music. This, of course, is because I have shown Alice that I have some degree of appreciation for the beauty and wonder of music which, like God, is a mystery. How does it work? Why does it work? We know that great music is saying something to us, but the message, though simple, is beyond words—like God's mysteries. Music has order, rhythm, pattern and yet freedom, unpredictability, novelty, beauty—like God. We talk for a long time about all this in the dream because there is a lot to say!

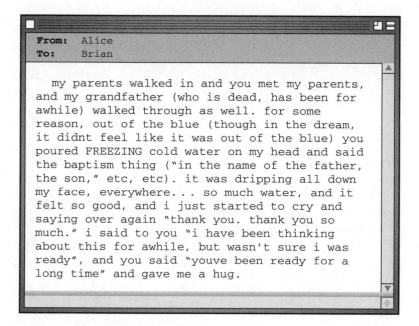

From: Alice
To: Brian

   my parents walked in and you met my parents,
and my grandfather (who is dead, has been for
awhile) walked through as well. for some
reason, out of the blue (though in the dream,
it didnt feel like it was out of the blue) you
poured FREEZING cold water on my head and said
the baptism thing ("in the name of the father,
the son," etc, etc). it was dripping all down
my face, everywhere... so much water, and it
felt so good, and i just started to cry and
saying over again "thank you. thank you so
much." i said to you "i have been thinking
about this for awhile, but wasn't sure i was
ready", and you said "youve been ready for a
long time" and gave me a hug.

The details about her parents walking in, along with her grandfather who died long ago, are pregnant and suggestive. What we are talking about is something that goes back to the ancient past—the world of our forefathers—and it goes beyond what we see and experience here and now, beyond this life, where her grandfather is now.

Then comes the surprise of the baptism, and even the coldness of the water adds a shiver of exhilaration to the moment. It is all about surprise, because in a sense, Alice is telling herself through this dream (as I interpret it, anyway) that she is more ready to believe than she realizes; she is surprising herself by her openness to God. It is clear that when she says "thank you, thank you so much" again and again, she is not talking to me, but to God. Just as cold water poured over your head would take your breath away, her breath is taken away by the wonder of discovering that she herself is coming into contact with God.

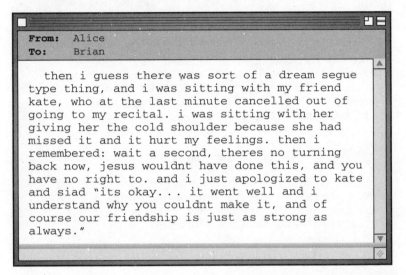

From: Alice
To: Brian

then i guess there was sort of a dream segue type thing, and i was sitting with my friend kate, who at the last minute cancelled out of going to my recital. i was sitting with her giving her the cold shoulder because she had missed it and it hurt my feelings. then i remembered: wait a second, theres no turning back now, jesus wouldnt have done this, and you have no right to. and i just apologized to kate and siad "its okay. . . it went well and i understand why you couldnt make it, and of course our friendship is just as strong as always."

Then the "dream segue" happens, and what an unexpected, but yet perfect, turn of events follows with her friend. The recital that my family was able to attend was the same one her friend missed, and this hurt Alice. But fresh on the heels of coming into contact with God (and again, the sensuousness of the cold water pouring down her becomes a metaphor for an almost tangible contact, doesn't it?) comes the awareness that she should act as Jesus would act, because being a follower of Jesus (which is what baptism signifies) means "no turning back now," and because she is forgiven it is impossible for her not to also forgive. So she forgives and reconciles, echoing the teachings of Jesus (which she has been reading for a few months now) in profound ways. It all comes together—our spiritual friendship, her own reading of the Scriptures, and the Holy Spirit's moving in her heart, her soul.

No wonder she wakes up feeling on the verge of "happy tears." You will notice that I am not saying that Alice was "born again," saved, or converted through this experience. And I am not saying that she wasn't. I used to worry a lot about this kind of spiritual diagnosis (Is he in yet? Is she one of us yet?), but my experience in evangelism and my reflections on the Scriptures have pushed me away from needing to have everything nailed down and everyone properly categorized and sorted. As Jesus said, the wind blows mysteriously; we can hear it but can't see it, and it is the same way with the Spirit. We know if the wind has blown because we see and hear the trees sway, and with Alice, we will know whether she has indeed encountered and connected with God by the results that we see and hear in her life. A dream, an emotion, even an affirmation of a doctrine or creed—all of these fall short of what Jesus told us really mattered: "By their fruit you shall know them," or "By this everyone will know you are my disciples ... by your love for one another." With Alice, the signs have been positive.

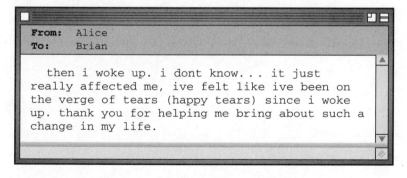

From: Alice
To: Brian

then i woke up. i dont know... it just really affected me, ive felt like ive been on the verge of tears (happy tears) since i woke up. thank you for helping me bring about such a change in my life.

Alice says some nice things about me in this email, complimenting the content and delivery of my messages, for example, and thanking me for helping her. But to me, the most powerful and affirming of her compliments is that I had a role in her dream, the role of believing in her more than she believed in herself, of baptizing her before she knew she was ready to be baptized. What an honor! What an honor to be a spiritual friend! I wish I could convey to you what I feel as I ponder this. More, I hope you will be inspired to dance and invite others into the dance, so you will know exactly what I am talking about if you do not already.

14 | Event and Process

As I said in the previous chapter, I am less preoccupied with dating a conversion event these days. Instead, I am more focused on being part of an ongoing process. But what do we call that process? And what is that process about?

In my early years as a Christian, I was taught to be event-oriented. There was an event—we variously called it accepting Christ as your personal Savior, getting saved, being born again, becoming a Christian—that was datable and time-able down to the minute, and this event was all-important. It was so important that everything that came after the event was seen as a sort of denouement. The term for it, "follow-up," suggested it was like cleaning up after a party, less exciting, less important than the focal point. If one could not tell his story (called a "testimony"), giving the precise date and time of one's conversion event, one's status as a Christian was suspect.

I would probably still see things this way today if it weren't for a number of experiences and realizations.

1. In my own experience, I am not sure exactly when my conversion happened. Because I grew up in churches that emphasized "getting saved," at the end of nearly every sermon I would pray, "God, if I'm not saved yet, let me be

saved now. If I wasn't sincere the last time, I want to be sincere this time." Which time "took"? I remember as a boy going to a special children's service and being especially "sincere" in my prayer for God to forgive my sins and save me. I came home and told my mother that I was now saved, but she tells me that some time before this event, she had noticed that on the back of a plaster plaque hanging on my wall (the kinds of plaques that kids would make in Christian summer camps or vacation Bible schools) that I had written, in pencil, "I know I'm saved." Although I have no memory of writing on the back of that plaque, it is clear that "crossing the line" was a preoccupation of my boyhood mind, conscience, and imagination. Later, in my teenage years, I had several profound and powerful spiritual experiences that were so transforming that I wondered if any of my childhood prayers had "counted" at all. When was I saved? God knows. I don't.

2. In college, I remember reading the spiritual autobiography of Jonathan Edwards, the leader of the Second Great Awakening in New England in the eighteenth century. Here was this great Christian leader who recounts a series of spiritual experiences but never identifies one of them as "the one." That was the first time I wondered if the "one-time event focus" may itself be flawed.

3. Meanwhile, I had become involved with the charismatic movement, and in these more Pentecostal circles, it was clear that one needed not one event, but two. Being "born again" or "saved" was a nice start, but have you been "baptized in the Spirit" or "filled with the Spirit"—have you received the *second* blessing? I realized that I could reinterpret my experience to fit their paradigm (and I later had more spiritual

experiences that also could fit their paradigm), and then I began to wonder if people simply interpret a wide range of experiences to fit into the expected formula of the group to which they wish to belong. That thought bothered me and in a way frightened me (I didn't want the world to get that complicated), but it wouldn't go away.

4. When I became more involved in church leadership, I participated for a while in something called Evangelism Explosion. This approach to evangelism was focused entirely on bringing people to a conversion event where they acknowledge a certain theory of the atonement and where they say a certain kind of prayer. I led many people through this prayer and rejoiced that they were "saved." But this method was flawed: Over time, I noticed that those who said the prayer the first time they were invited to almost never would be seen again in church. On the other hand, those who resisted or argued or just weren't ready continued coming back to church and asking questions and learning over time. The first group seemed to "get saved" without staying saved, and the second group seemed to stay saved without ever getting saved. These people, whose ongoing growth seemed to validate their genuine identity as followers of Christ, generally couldn't point back to any single event of "getting saved." Why not? This pattern frustrated me.

5. Years later I served on the board of a wonderful mission agency called International Teams (IT). One summer I visited IT missionaries across Europe, and, in case after case, I'd ask, "How's the work here going?" and they'd say something like "It's going great. The church we're working with is really growing. More and more people are coming to Christ. But, it is confusing. It used to be that you could

point to a specific day when they accepted Christ. Now it seems more like they come to church, get involved, learn, grow, and a year later, it's clear they've become Christians but nobody knows when." They were noticing the same trend I had noticed. What was going on?

For all of these reasons and more, I have let go my focus on "punctiliar salvation," a preoccupation with an event or point at which a person "gets it." In fact, I came up with a little diagram to show various processes by which people seem to come to Christian faith and commitment.

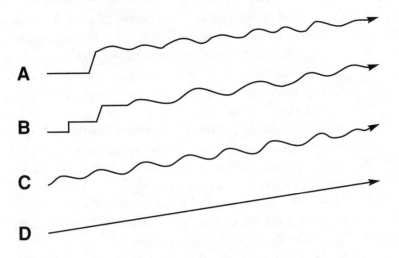

Line A represents the "punctiliar salvation" focus. One is born "dead in trespasses and sins," with no spiritual life, nothing happening between one's soul and God. At some point (perhaps during childhood or adolescence, or perhaps after a terrible crisis or personal failure in adulthood), one turns to God, is born again, and a new life begins.

Line B represents the Pentecostal or charismatic focus. As in Line A, one is born and does not grow spiritually until one is born again, and then one lives at a higher but stagnant level until one is filled with or baptized in the Holy Spirit. Then one begins to grow.

Line C represents a more Catholic or mainline Protestant view. One is born and raised in the "training and instruction of the Lord." At various times, one experiences ups and downs spiritually. There may be defining moments (like confirmation) and turning points along the way, but basically life is seen as a gradual spiritual growth process, and no single conversion event is expected.

Line D represents the person who says, "I have always believed in and loved God." I used to think that people who said this were being dishonest, until I thought about John the Baptist, who was described by Luke as being filled with the Holy Spirit from his mother's womb (Luke 1:15). In other words, his infant capacity was filled with God, and his toddler capacity was similarly filled with God, and so on, until full adulthood, when he continued to live in the fullness of a relationship with God. Perhaps John was a rare or unique case, but his example opens up this possibility.

Looking back at Alice's experience, which line would you use to describe her experience? Or do you even need to try to graph her spiritual progress? This brings us to a key insight into spiritual friendship: *Rather than requiring people to fit into one of these categories, a spiritual friend tries to discern which is happening and to encourage the process.*

This is not to say that spiritual friends are ignorant of the importance of events when, in fact, the opposite is true. In this regard, I think back to my days as a college instructor. My wife and I lived just off campus, and on Thursday nights we started a fellowship group that welcomed both committed Christians and uncommitted spiritual seekers for an hour of Bible study, discussion, singing, and prayer. Marie, one of my former students, began attending, and she showed real interest. After the meeting one night, I was talking to her while people were mingling around our apartment, enjoying some refreshments.

I asked her, "Marie, where would you say you are in relation to God right now? Are you out on the street looking at God's house? Are you walking up the sidewalk? Are you knocking on the front door? Or, are you inside and part of the family?" There is no right or wrong answer to this question. It is a question that helps a person locate himself or herself on the spiritual journey. (I sometimes ask a question similar to this: "How would you describe your relationship to God at this point? Are you strangers, acquaintances, dating, engaged, happily married, unhappily married, separated, divorced, or something in between?" These kinds of questions seem to help people help me know how to help them. By telling me where they are in the process, they help me know how to help them take the next step. "Helping people take the next step" is a great way to define spiritual friendship, wouldn't you agree?)

This kind of question made sense to ask at this time because Marie and I had been conversing about her spiritual life for several months. I knew that she came from a religious family, but had rejected Christianity upon entering college and had considered herself an atheist for a few years. But she felt that atheism left her without meaning or hope, and she had begun feeling a kind of spiritual emptiness. As my student, she sensed that I was a "spiritual person," which encouraged her to talk to me after class and get better acquainted. She told me that her boyfriend, with whom she lived, wasn't interested in spirituality, but that she was. When I told her about our Thursday night group, she said she would like to come.

So I felt comfortable asking this question, knowing that she had been coming on Thursday nights for several weeks now, learning more about God, the Bible, Jesus, and what it would mean to be a Christian. Marie said, "I guess I'm knocking at the front door, wondering how to get in."

At that moment, I knew that an "event" was ready to happen. I asked her, "Would you like me to help you take the next step inside?"

Her eyes brimmed with tears, and she said, "Yes. I was hoping someone would help me. I feel like I want to come in, but I don't know what to do."

I then felt God's Spirit nudging me to invite others to be part of the event that was about to occur. (This too is an essential element of spiritual friendship—being sensitive to God's Spirit, who guides us in what to say and do through what some people call "promptings"—or what I'm here calling a "nudge." Not a great theological term, but I think you get the idea.)

I asked Marie if she'd mind the whole group being part of this, and she said that it would be fine. Obviously, she had a high degree of confidence in me that I wouldn't embarrass her or do anything "weird"—a confidence built through our spiritual friendship over several months. So I got everyone's attention and asked them to sit down again, and I explained, "Marie would like to become part of God's family tonight. So I thought we all could be part of welcoming her in. Marie, I'd like to lead you in a prayer that you can either pray out loud or silently after me, whichever you prefer. Okay?" She agreed and preferred to pray silently. Then we all bowed our heads, and I invited those who were sitting close by to lay their hands on Marie and pray for her. Then I prayed, "God, I want to be part of your family. I want to change the direction of my life to love you with all my heart and love other people as myself. I want to be a follower of Your Son, Jesus, for all the days of my life. . . . Marie, if there's anything else you want to say, just say it now, and when you're done, let us know by saying 'amen.' And everyone, be praying for Marie right now." When she said "amen," everyone applauded and got in line to give her a hug, and that marked the beginning of her new life as a follower of Christ.

For another friend, the event occurred at church one Sunday. At Cedar Ridge, we celebrate communion each week, and we do it Catholic- or Episcopal-style, with people coming forward to receive the bread and wine. Marv had been coming to Cedar Ridge for a few months, having been invited by his teenage daughter. When he heard I enjoyed the outdoors, he invited me to take a hike with him sometime at a nearby park, which gave us a chance to begin a spiritual friendship. At that point, he told me he didn't believe in God, but was learning a lot and getting closer to faith. I encouraged him to keep coming and to let me know if I could do anything for him. Each Sunday, when people came forward for communion, he would remain in his seat, because he understood that communion was an expression of faith in and commitment to Christ—something he didn't share. But then, one Sunday, I noticed he came forward. He caught my eye on his way back to his seat and walked over and gave me a "high five"—his way of saying that he had passed an important milestone. I hope for Marv, every Sunday as he takes communion, he will be reaffirming the decision he "went public" with that day. In fact, I hope that is how every Christian experiences communion.

So, yes, there are conversion events, but these events are better seen as milestones in an ongoing process. While this process model may seem like a departure from the traditional focus on the conversion event familiar to many evangelicals, Robert Webber's *Journey to Jesus* (Abingdon, 2001) makes clear that the process model of conversion is in fact an ancient and orthodox idea, not a new or heterodox one. In the early centuries of the church, he explains, a four-stage process became normative. The four stages of the process (seeker, hearer, kneeler, and faithful) were marked by milestone events or rites of passage, thus synthesizing the values of both event and process models.

In all of these ways, we celebrate milestone events in the spiritual journey. But we keep the conversion event rooted in its proper context—a process of spiritual growth and change. If the process "works," the events will happen. Without the process, the events may be illusory, meaningless, appearances without reality.

15 | The Whole Cosmic Theological Equation

Whatever happened when Alice had her "baptism dream" (back in chapter 12), it was not the end of the process. It was not the beginning either. It was a milestone in her ongoing discipleship. A few months later, she participated in a planning retreat for our contemplative prayer service. After the retreat, I received this email from her:

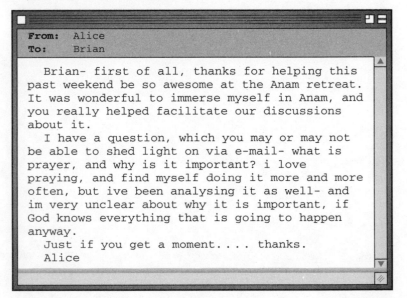

From: Alice
To: Brian

Brian- first of all, thanks for helping this past weekend be so awesome at the Anam retreat. It was wonderful to immerse myself in Anam, and you really helped facilitate our discussions about it.
I have a question, which you may or may not be able to shed light on via e-mail- what is prayer, and why is it important? i love praying, and find myself doing it more and more often, but ive been analysing it as well- and im very unclear about why it is important, if God knows everything that is going to happen anyway.
Just if you get a moment.... thanks.
Alice

First, I think it is fascinating for Alice to write "I love praying, and I find myself doing it more and more often." This is as it should be: our experience coming first, and then our reflection— she calls it "analyzing"—following. I replied to Alice's question, and she included my answer in her reply.

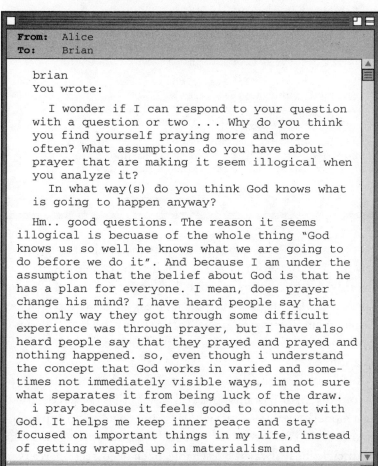

From: Alice
To: Brian

brian
You wrote:

  I wonder if I can respond to your question with a question or two ... Why do you think you find yourself praying more and more often? What assumptions do you have about prayer that are making it seem illogical when you analyze it?
  In what way(s) do you think God knows what is going to happen anyway?

Hm.. good questions. The reason it seems illogical is becuase of the whole thing "God knows us so well he knows what we are going to do before we do it". And because I am under the assumption that the belief about God is that he has a plan for everyone. I mean, does prayer change his mind? I have heard people say that the only way they got through some difficult experience was through prayer, but I have also heard people say that they prayed and prayed and nothing happened. so, even though i understand the concept that God works in varied and some-times not immediately visible ways, im not sure what separates it from being luck of the draw.
  i pray because it feels good to connect with God. It helps me keep inner peace and stay focused on important things in my life, instead of getting wrapped up in materialism and

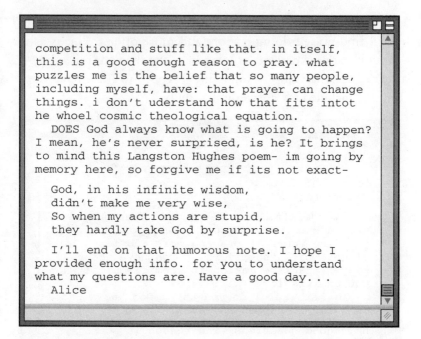

competition and stuff like that. in itself,
this is a good enough reason to pray. what
puzzles me is the belief that so many people,
including myself, have: that prayer can change
things. i don't uderstand how that fits intot
he whoel cosmic theological equation.
   DOES God always know what is going to happen?
I mean, he's never surprised, is he? It brings
to mind this Langston Hughes poem- im going by
memory here, so forgive me if its not exact-

   God, in his infinite wisdom,
   didn't make me very wise,
   So when my actions are stupid,
   they hardly take God by surprise.

   I'll end on that humorous note. I hope I
provided enough info. for you to understand
what my questions are. Have a good day...
   Alice

I thought this email was a good one to include because it makes clear that part of spiritual friendship is helping people put together a worldview, a web or mosaic of belief, a pattern that makes sense. I love Alice's language: "what puzzles me is the belief that so many people, including myself, have: that prayer can change things. i don't understand how that fits into the whole cosmic theological equation."

Realize that spirituality isn't just about beliefs about God, or sin, or heaven, or morality. In a real way, faith is about constructing a model of reality—"the whole cosmic theological equation," as Alice says. This is why faith must always be growing, and why the disciple must always be teachable, open to correction, ready to admit "I'm wrong," and ready to think again (the root meaning of "repent"). This is because none of us is so naïve as to believe that he or she has the whole cosmic theological equation figured out. Nobody's model is perfect. We are constantly in the process of critiquing our model, adjusting it, recalibrating it. Alice captures this perfectly when she says that she is puzzled by a belief that many people—including herself—hold. This, to me, is a wonderful sign of wisdom and growth—to hold beliefs that puzzle you, and to be puzzled by beliefs that you hold. This is the vital sign of a vibrant faith of heart and head, a dynamic faith that isn't brain-dead, hasn't committed intellectual suicide, and is in process.

So I think it is an essential dimension of spiritual friendship to help one another do this puzzling, analyzing, reflecting. You will notice that I answered her original question not with easy answers but with some more questions (a facet of spiritual friendship that we have seen again and again) to help her think even deeper. After this second message on the subject of prayer and "the whole cosmic theological equation," I did offer some of my reflections. I copied her previous message into my response, which, for once, I saved.

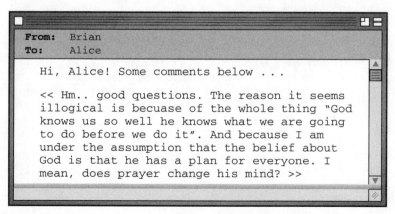

From: Brian
To: Alice

Hi, Alice! Some comments below . . .

<< Hm.. good questions. The reason it seems illogical is becuase of the whole thing "God knows us so well he knows what we are going to do before we do it". And because I am under the assumption that the belief about God is that he has a plan for everyone. I mean, does prayer change his mind? >>

I think one of the ways modernity has influenced Christianity is by imposing a deterministic, mechanistic worldview onto it. I think a Christian belief is that God is all-powerful ... but that doesn't mean that God "makes" everything happen or "controls" everything that happens. I think it's safe to say that the universe is never "out of control" (i.e. God can't stop it, intervene, etc.) ... but that doesn't mean that everything that happens in it is controlled. Does that make sense? Here's how I try to explain it sometimes: God is so powerful that he could create a universe of free creatures that have real power of their own. God is so powerful that he can make beings that aren't just automatons or mechanisms or puppets or robots.

If that's the case ... then God's "mind" or "will" is to create an interactive universe, not where he has his mind made up and we change it, but one in which we all interact with one another and with him. Prayer makes a lot of sense in that kind of universe ... but as an interpersonal, not mechanistic, interaction. This is exactly what you say below....

<< I have heard people say that the only way they got through some difficult experience was through prayer, but I have also heard people say that they prayed and prayed and nothing happened. so, even though i understand the concept that God works in varied and sometimes not immediately visible ways, im not sure what sperates it from being luck of the draw. >>

Yes, if our focus is on "getting our way," then prayer is a pretty frustrating experience. But if the focus is on getting connected and

staying connected to God . . . that's a very
different (and more appropriate, I think)
approach to prayer. Does that make sense? It's
exactly as you say below . . .

<< i pray because it feels good to connect
with God. It helps me keep inner peace and
stay focused on important things in my life,
instead of getting wrapped up in materialism
and competition and stuff like that. in
itself, this is a good enough reason to pray.
what puzzles me is the belief that so many
people, including myself, have: that prayer
can change things. i don't uderstand how that
fits intot he whoel cosmic theological
equation. >>

Here again, I think it's a both/and rather
than either/or. I don't know if you're free the
first Tuesday of February, but the Science and
Faith group at Cedar Ridge is going to discuss
this very issue, regarding whether and how God
can intervene in the universe. It's based on C.
S. Lewis wonderful book, "Miracles."

<< DOES God always know what is going to
happen? I mean, he's never surprised, is he?
It brings to mind this Langston Hughes poem-
im going by memory here, so forgive me if its
not exact-

God, in his infinite wisdom,
didn't make me very wise,
So when my actions are stupid,
they hardly take God by surprise.

I'll end on that humorous note. I hope I
provided enough info. for you to understand
what my questions are. Have a good day. . . >>

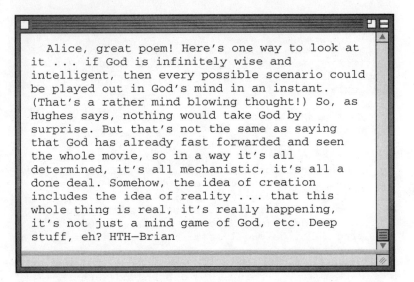

Alice, great poem! Here's one way to look at it . . . if God is infinitely wise and intelligent, then every possible scenario could be played out in God's mind in an instant. (That's a rather mind blowing thought!) So, as Hughes says, nothing would take God by surprise. But that's not the same as saying that God has already fast forwarded and seen the whole movie, so in a way it's all determined, it's all mechanistic, it's all a done deal. Somehow, the idea of creation includes the idea of reality . . . that this whole thing is real, it's really happening, it's not just a mind game of God, etc. Deep stuff, eh? HTH—Brian

You may disagree with my response, and, in fact, I may be wrong. After all, I'm just a disciple myself, learning and growing and changing my model of the universe as I go. But I hope you can see that I am not trying to impose my thinking on Alice; instead, I am trying to be a spiritual friend, sharing my thinking to help as it may.

16 | I Don't Understand. Sorry to Bombard You

Actually, I think that last email confused Alice a little, and maybe even troubled her. So, here was how she responded, followed by my response:

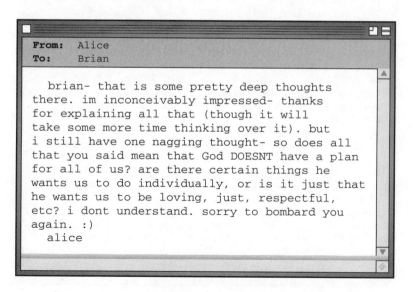

From: Alice
To: Brian

brian- that is some pretty deep thoughts
there. im inconceivably impressed- thanks
for explaining all that (though it will
take some more time thinking over it). but
i still have one nagging thought- so does all
that you said mean that God DOESNT have a plan
for all of us? are there certain things he
wants us to do individually, or is it just that
he wants us to be loving, just, respectful,
etc? i dont understand. sorry to bombard you
again. :)
  alice

From: Brian
To: Alice

Hi, Alice—

You wrote—

<< but i still have one nagging thought- so does all that you said mean that God DOESNT have a plan for all of us? are there certain things he wants us to do individually, or is it just that he wants us to be loving, just, respectful, etc? i dont understand. sorry to bombard you again. :) >>

Alice—these are really deep waters, so I'm sure I'm not going to resolve all the mysteries of the universe! But this analogy works for me . . . My daughter Rachel is in college. I definitely have a plan for her, and I am always available for her, and everything I have is at her disposal . . . but part of my plan is for her to have her own life, a real life of her own. I wanted her to choose a college, to choose a major, to develop her own friends, etc. I don't want her to use drugs, abuse sex, be selfish, etc., etc. . . . but I don't want to try to control her either. I think God's workings with us are very similar. He really wants us to have freedom, but he also wants what is best for us . . . .

If Rachel comes to me and asks for advice, I'll give it to her. On some things she might ask about, I might have no opinion—like should she order Caesar Salad or Bean Soup for dinner? Whatever! On other things, I'll have REALLY clear guidance for her . . . like should she marry this guy who's insecure and selfish and unstable, or that guy who's kind and stable and committed to God?

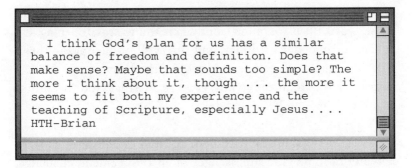

I think God's plan for us has a similar balance of freedom and definition. Does that make sense? Maybe that sounds too simple? The more I think about it, though ... the more it seems to fit both my experience and the teaching of Scripture, especially Jesus. ...
HTH-Brian

Of course, the conversation has continued, and continues to this day. Eventually, I think we will move beyond the mode where I am always in the teacher role and Alice is always in the student role. I imagine we will arrive at a moment like one I remember, sitting in an old ugly Datsun in the 1970s with one of my first spiritual friends.

In that spiritual friendship, I had been the student and Dave had been the mentor. He taught me so much, and modeled spiritual friendship in ways that I am still reflecting on and learning from. Sometimes he really surprised me, like the time at my high school graduation party when he pulled me aside and said, "Well, Brian, I just wanted to congratulate you. I mean, not only have you graduated from high school, but you've also arrived spiritually." (At this point, I remember making a surprised face. What?) "Seriously, Brian ... you know more about the Bible than most people. You can lead a Bible study, give your testimony, answer most of the questions people will ask you. You really have learned all anybody will expect you to know for the rest of your life. You've arrived. You don't need to grow any more." Then I realized he was joking, and we both had a laugh.

Then he became serious and said, "Really, Brian, I want you to remember that you'll never stop growing in Christ. I don't ever want you to get comfortable. I want you to always find the curl of the wave, the place out in front where things are happening. Go to the cutting edge of things, and throw your energies in there. That's where you belong." Now, nearly thirty years later, I remember that moment vividly, and I realize that God was speaking to me through Dave that day.

What an awesome dimension of spiritual friendship that is, to actually become God's messenger of encouragement, challenge, and direction. And sometimes, of warning or correction, which brings back another memory of Dave's spiritual friendship.

Dave was one of the "adult" leaders for the youth group I was part of. I have added quotes around "adult" since he was in college at the time, just five or six years older than me. We were finishing a weekend retreat, loading suitcases into the back of an old bus. Dave pulled me aside and said, "Can we talk for a minute?"

I said, "Sure!" I was in a great mood. I can't remember anything about the retreat spiritually, but I had a blast. The prettiest girl in the youth group had brought along a friend of hers, equally pretty, and the three of us had hung out together all weekend. My only problem was that I couldn't figure out which of the girls I had a bigger crush on!

We walked across the parking lot (actually, I was kind of floating), and Dave shocked me and ended my elation fast: "Brian, I'm really disappointed in you."

What? What?! Why?

"All weekend, you've been hanging out with the two prettiest girls on the retreat."

Yes, I'd noticed! What's wrong with that?

"Brian, I want you to think about all the less beautiful girls who came on this retreat. Everywhere else in their lives—at school, on the streets, on TV, in the movies, in magazines—they're told that it is the pretty girls that count. I was kind of hoping it would be different here. You know? I was hoping that among followers of Christ, there wouldn't be favoritism shown to pretty and popular people. I was thinking that in our youth group, everyone would find one place in the world where everybody is accepted and loved. That's why I'm really disappointed."

I remember feeling a mixture of sorrow and anger. Anger—who was he to . . . ? Sorrow—he was right. So guess who I *didn't* sit with on the bus ride on the way home? And guess who has always remembered that it is often the shyest people, the least attractive or popular or socially confident people, who most need and deserve my time and attention?

Dave and I had been through a lot leading up to that afternoon sitting in his dumpy old Datsun. Here's what he said to me: "Brian, today marks a kind of change in our friendship. You see, up until now, I've been discipling you. I've been trying to help you grow. But I feel that now you have learned everything I have to teach you. I feel like you're now my peer. In fact, I think in the future, I'll learn as much from you as you've leaned from me."

And of course, in saying that, he was teaching me something I'm still learning: Christian spiritual friendship is always about encouragement, empowerment, believing in people, whether we do so from "up ahead" as mentors, from beside as peers, or even "from behind" as students ourselves. It is not a matter of status at all. How could it be otherwise, considering Jesus, who washed his disciples' feet, took the role of a servant, and told his disciples they would do greater things than he did?

This strikes me as one of the most unexpected lessons of the Gospels—Jesus believes in people. Of course, on the one hand, he knows what we are made of, and he doesn't cherish any illusions about how strong our flesh is, even when our spirits are willing. But on the other hand, it is amazing how much Jesus entrusts to us.

While preparing for a sermon recently, I did a computer search on the word *trust* in the Gospels, expecting to find a lot of passages about our need to trust God. What I found, though, was the more common word *entrust*—my computer turned those up too. I started noticing how many stories Jesus told about people being entrusted with things—wealth, duty, and responsibility. And I realized that this was what Dave was saying to me that day: "I trust you, brother. I trust you to keep learning, keep growing, to keep doing good, and keep doing well. I believe in you and know that you'll do greater things than I have." And in this way, Dave was demonstrating Christ's own friendship, because along with the trust came the promise of his ongoing friendship, something that continues to this day. Anytime I need a friend, I know I can call Dave. What an example he has been!

And Brent, and Rod, and another Dave, and Todd, and Chuck, and Rich, and so many others.

Perhaps this is why I want to encourage you to be a spiritual friend to others. Not just in the church, but especially outside it—to live by the music of the gospel and help others hear it and join the dance too.

17 | It's Because I Feel a Little of God's Love

Months have passed since the last email, and the volume of correspondence between Alice and me has gradually decreased. That is as it should be. She has many other spiritual friends now, and she is growing in faith in many wonderful ways. She has had her setbacks, though. Once she came to see me, discouraged about her spiritual progress. The "surging and receding" of her faith continued to bother her. For a while, she was comparing herself to others that she met in the music team at church. They always seemed so strong spiritually; they always seemed to enjoy leading the church in worship so much. Sometimes, she told me, when she played for the church, she was just playing. It was like any other gig. This disturbed her. What was wrong with her? Why didn't she feel what everyone else seemed to feel?

I assured her that I knew the others on the team very well, and I was certain that each of them had their ups and downs too. The difference was that they had been following Christ longer, and they had learned to accept these vacillations in their faith-feelings as inevitable, just as married people learn that their marriage is more secure when they depend on their commitment, not their feelings, which rise and fall from day to day.

She didn't seem very satisfied with this at first, but it was the best I could offer her; however, Alice recently told me that this conversation was more important than I realized. From it she realized that she didn't need to compare herself with others and consider them the norm and herself the oddity.

I was nearly finished with this manuscript one Saturday not long ago when I got this message from her. (By the way, I don't think there is any connection with her spiritual progress and her discovery of the joys of capitalization!)

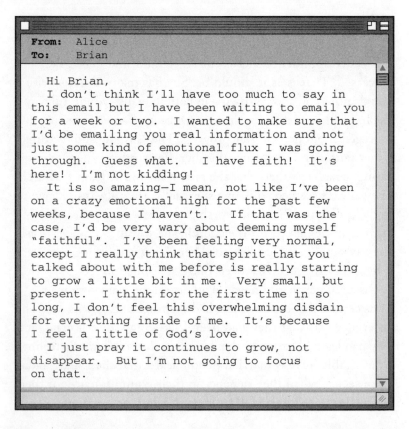

From: Alice
To: Brian

Hi Brian,
I don't think I'll have too much to say in this email but I have been waiting to email you for a week or two. I wanted to make sure that I'd be emailing you real information and not just some kind of emotional flux I was going through. Guess what. I have faith! It's here! I'm not kidding!
It is so amazing—I mean, not like I've been on a crazy emotional high for the past few weeks, because I haven't. If that was the case, I'd be very wary about deeming myself "faithful". I've been feeling very normal, except I really think that spirit that you talked about with me before is really starting to grow a little bit in me. Very small, but present. I think for the first time in so long, I don't feel this overwhelming disdain for everything inside of me. It's because I feel a little of God's love.
I just pray it continues to grow, not disappear. But I'm not going to focus on that.

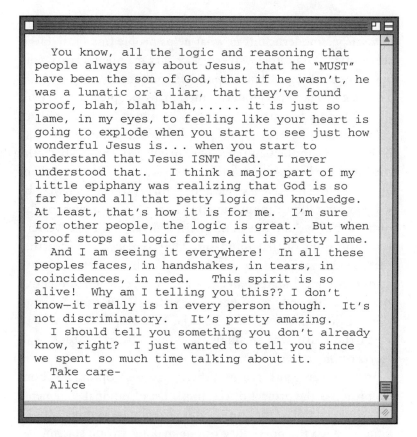

You know, all the logic and reasoning that people always say about Jesus, that he "MUST" have been the son of God, that if he wasn't, he was a lunatic or a liar, that they've found proof, blah, blah blah,..... it is just so lame, in my eyes, to feeling like your heart is going to explode when you start to see just how wonderful Jesus is... when you start to understand that Jesus ISNT dead. I never understood that. I think a major part of my little epiphany was realizing that God is so far beyond all that petty logic and knowledge. At least, that's how it is for me. I'm sure for other people, the logic is great. But when proof stops at logic for me, it's pretty lame.

And I am seeing it everywhere! In all these peoples faces, in handshakes, in tears, in coincidences, in need. This spirit is so alive! Why am I telling you this?? I don't know—it really is in every person though. It's not discriminatory. It's pretty amazing.

I should tell you something you don't already know, right? I just wanted to tell you since we spent so much time talking about it.

Take care-
Alice

Perhaps you can read that message without a smile sneaking onto your face, but I can't. As Alice said, "It's pretty amazing."

Once again, I'm struck by both her insight and her expression: "when proof stops at logic for me, it's pretty lame." This is yet another way that Alice shows herself to be a postmodern person. She's right: For some people—especially modern ones—the "lord, lunatic, or liar" logic "is great." But for her, proof has to go beyond logic.

In my other books, I have tried in various ways to explain this modern/postmodern shift in what helps people find faith. Here, let me offer yet another way—a way that may help clarify why logic-plus-nothing is "lame" for Alice and those like her.

If we go back to premodern times, many people believed (this is hard for us to imagine, much less understand) that truth resided in people, in groups—people like the pope, groups like the Roman Catholic Church. These privileged people "had" the truth, and the best way to get the truth was to trust and consult those people. The Renaissance and Reformation (which may be two ways of talking about the same larger phenomenon, one in southern Europe and one in northern Europe) knocked Western civilization out of that mind-set. They replaced the idea that truth resides in people or institutions with a belief that truth resides in logical statements, abstract propositions, objective concepts independent of people, existing "out there" some- where. In this new way of seeing the universe, the best way to get to the truth was through thinking, research, study—all efforts of the individual.

By the seventeenth century, there was great optimism about this project—the project of creating a list of rational statements that would comprise the truth about virtually everything. But all acknowledged the possibility of one making wrong statements. How could one be sure that wrong statements didn't enter into one's thinking?

The solution was elegant: One must doubt everything and remove all possible errors. Then, if even just one single undoubtable certainty remained standing, one could build upon that foundation of certainty a structure of knowledge that was as certain as its foundation. This, of course, is contingent upon the fact that one proceeded with impeccable rational logic from the existing premise to new conclusion, which would in turn become the new premise for the next conclusion, and so on.

This way of thinking, this project of achieving what Mike Regele has called "bombproof certainty" about virtually everything, has been called variously "the Enlightenment project" and "foundationalism." The latter is a useful term because it presents the dominant metaphor of the Enlightenment project: Truth is a system of propositions, laid like bricks and cemented by logic, resting on the foundation of indubitable and self-evident truths. And the word "resting" is significant as well: The goal of foundationalism is a kind of rest, where everything is settled, questions are answered, doubts are removed, knowledge is *known.*

By the middle of the twentieth century, when confidence in the Enlightenment project was, on the popular level, at its apogee, among many philosophers, the foundations of foundationalism were crumbling. In Europe, with the tragedy of the Holocaust as real and unforgettable as the bombed out buildings and military graveyards visible everywhere, there was this haunting fear that if our Enlightenment project were truly so wonderful, how could it lead us to this? Deep in the European psyche was this unshakeable feeling that Western civilization—the bearers of the Enlightenment torch—had failed, and so foundationalism was discredited with it.

Meanwhile, in the U.S., philosophers like W. V. Quine and later Thomas Kuhn, Peter Berger, Susan Haak, and others began suggesting that the image of the wall or building resting on a solid foundation was not accurate. They said that the way people in real life develop their belief systems isn't nearly so neat or simple. Quine said that belief systems are more like a spider's web than a wall. Beliefs are connections we make, like a spider's strands, linking one observation to another, or linking one link between observations and other links. Rather than resting in sweet certainty, he suggested, real-life beliefs tend to hang in dynamic tension. Beliefs were always being plucked or stretched or even broken like the strands of a web, and people were always seeking to mend tears and bolster sags and cover holes.

Philosophers after Quine suggested that even his metaphor was too sanguine. Really, they said, we hold our beliefs like little fragments of webs, loosely connected if at all. None of us as individuals or as societies can pretend to have all-encompassing webs of belief, but rather, we possess our little areas of expertise, which cover tiny areas of a vast space of ignorance or bewilderment. Other metaphors suggested themselves: We are like castaways riding rickety rafts of logs at sea, but our rafts continually fall apart; we are constantly standing on a few logs trying to relash others, rebuilding our rafts while we ride them. Or yet again, we ride our rafts in little flotillas, and as one raft disintegrates, we jump onto another, and from it we seek to repair the first, but meanwhile, a third raft has begun to fall apart, so we quickly have to turn our attentions there. Or, our worldviews are like complex crossword puzzles, requiring us to fit new hypotheses within the spaces created by previous conclusions. Sometimes, when a new hypothesis that we're confident in just won't fit in with existing conclusions, we have to go back and erase or revise our previous "knowledge."

These metaphors are far less sanguine about humanity's ability to fully understand the cosmos or ourselves with simple answers and absolute certainty. One imagines a great scientist or philosopher pondering the disintegration of modern foundationalism. At his feet sits his golden retriever, looking up at him with canine affection. "You poor dog," he mumbles. "You think you understand me, and in a small way, you do. But even though you know me in your own way, you can know nothing about the magic of poetry, or the delicacy of a fine wine, or the pathos of Mozart, or the wonder of nuclear fusion, or the grand simplicity of DNA." And then he reaches down and pats the dog sympathetically, looks into his brown eyes, and says, "And now I realize that my pretensions to completely understand anything, much less everything, including myself . . . are no more realistic than you thinking you fully understand me."

There is sadness in that moment—the sadness of the end of the modern era, I think. But there is also humility in that moment, as the man reaches down and pats his dog's side with a poignant sympathy; his touch is almost fraternal, no longer patronizing. And that humility provides a new opening for faith, which is one of the reasons I believe that spiritual friendships are so important these days!

When Alice talks about the "lameness" of logic, I think it is this larger Enlightenment foundationalism she is critiquing. Some of my readers, perhaps most, will feel uneasy with her critique, because although it is never spoken of, hardly ever noticed, to a great degree modern Christianity has bought into foundationalism as much as or perhaps more than the secular culture at large. True, our "foundation" may be different, but our dream is the same: Achieving a bombproof certainty, a state of faith where all our beliefs are at rest, where everything is proven logically, where there is no dynamic tension, where everything is clear and clean and unwrinkled and in its place, like pressed shirts in a suitcase.

I think Alice may be ahead of many of us, including many of us who have been raised in the church and consider ourselves "pew-time" veterans with theological credentials more like those of the scientist than of the golden retriever in the previous paragraphs. This is because Alice has embarked on a path where her faith is not "at rest" through "proofs." Rather, on her path, faith is alive, moving, pulsing, swaying, each belief trembling in dynamic tension with the others. It is real faith—"Jesus ISN'T dead," she affirms. But it is less like a static system of belief, an interlocking wall of cemented-in certainties, and more like a passion, an adventure, a discovery, a wild wonder—"feeling like your heart is going to explode when you start to see just how wonderful Jesus is." Yet in spite of the passion, she is careful to distinguish it from some kind of "emotional flux": "I've been feeling very normal," she says.

What she is experiencing is nothing less than transformation, as is seen by the word *except,* and it is a humble transformation, shown in "a little bit ... very small, but present": "I've been feeling very normal, except I really think that spirit that you talked about with me before is really starting to grow a little bit in me. Very small, but present."

Furthermore, what she is experiencing is liberating, liberating in a way that surely inspires all of us to celebrate with her: "I think for the first time in so long, I don't feel this overwhelming disdain for everything inside of me. It's because I feel a little of God's love."

It has been nearly two years since I helped Alice load her harp into the back of her vehicle and responded to her question with the offer of a conversation. When I read those words, "I don't feel this overwhelming disdain for everything inside of me," and, "I feel a little of God's love," I thank God for the privilege and miracle of spiritual friendship. I think of Jesus, befriending a few men and women in Palestine, and sending them "to every nation" to spread the friendship (Paul called it a message of reconciliation) everywhere. I thank God for how that friendship, passing from person to person, across cultures and generations, from century to century, eventually reached me, and now it has reached Alice. And I think of the others who will be welcomed into the friendship through Alice, and through the spiritual friends Alice makes.

And I think of you, and I hope that you want to be part of this "pretty amazing" thing too. I hope you hear the music, and feel it moving you, and that you will help others hear it and love it and feel it like a song in the lungs and a dance in the limbs . . . and join this wonderful dance of God's "nondiscriminatory" love.

18 | This Overwhelming Disdain for Everything Inside of Me

When I reread Alice's words, "I think for the first time in so long, I don't feel this overwhelming disdain for everything inside of me," I am surprised—surprised in a sad way, because it breaks my heart to think that Alice carried around a sense of shame and guilt. Such a wonderful person, I think. She shouldn't feel this way! But really, Alice here expresses something we all identify with at some profound level, although many people suppress it and live superficially "above" it, like naïve swimmers frolicking with a shark cruising beneath them. As with Alice, our most profound need is to acknowledge the disdain and to "feel a little of God's love." To practice spiritual friendship, to make disciples, to evangelize—whatever we call it—cannot be put any more powerfully or poignantly than as liberation from "overwhelming disdain" of guilt and shame to a genuine experience of God's love.

So we reach the point in the book where I try to summarize what Alice has taught me about helping people feel a little of God's love. But I feel ambivalent. I have worked hard to avoid anything close to formulae or "easy steps"—for reasons that I hope are obvious to you by now. At the same time, I think it would be helpful to try to bring things together around eight factors—not easy steps, not formulae, but elements, factors, parts of a bigger whole that cannot be easily nailed down. Each factor may offer a way for us to review what we have considered together.

1. The Relational Factor: Count conversations, not just conversions.
Some of us Christians don't "get out much." We run from holy huddle to holy huddle, like squirrels darting from tree to tree, afraid that we will get hammered by a devil or seduced by a temptation. If you want to be that kind of Christian—a "church lady" whose virgin ears cannot stand the rough language of the street or a "Ned Flanders" type who really does seem to be a cartoon—then forget about spiritual friendship. You are not ready for it.

But if you are willing to get out, reach out, relate to and willing to be a neighbor, a friend, a decent human being, then you are more ready than you realize. It might be someone at work, a waitress where you have breakfast, the teenage son of a neighbor, your nephew, a person whose car you will see broken down at the side of the road later this week. You don't start by being religious; you start by being human, relational, neighborly, friendly. If you've forgotten, it is never too late to relearn.

You may have to, as we suggested before, trim back your church activities. Instead of yet another Bible study (how many more do you need?), you might start coaching basketball, or taking an art class, or volunteering at a retirement community, or tutoring at a neighborhood school—just to get out a bit. In the process you will meet some people and you will ask some questions, conversations will begin, and a relationship will develop. Don't worry about the content of the conversions. Just get them going and see what happens.

2. The Narrative Factor: Listen to their story, share your story, and share God's story, not just propositions or formulas.

As we have seen throughout this book, somewhere along the line modernity tricked us into thinking that the greatest truths are contained in abstractions rather than stories. Nonetheless, we are regaining perspective these days. So we start by honoring the stories around us.

Next time you are on an airplane, don't hurry to stand squashed in the center aisle waiting to deplane at your destination. Just sit there and look at the people. Notice their faces. Imagine the story behind each face—where they have come from, where they are going and why, whom they love and who loves them, what they want and need and dream about, what drives them and draws them. You can do the same waiting in line at the grocery store, sitting in the mall, or stopped in traffic. You are a story in progress surrounded by stories in progress, and at any moment, your story could intersect with the story of someone else, and as a result, both of your stories will take a novel turn. In the process, both of you will find yourselves part of God's unfolding story too, because God's story intersects with ours at every turn, in every breath, pulsing in every heartbeat.

3. The Communal Factor: Expect conversion to normally occur in the context of authentic Christian community, not just in the context of information.

Spiritual friendship isn't just about you. You are part of something bigger, something Paul called "the body of Christ." In a real way, Jesus is still here in the flesh, but now, instead of looking at the world through one pair of eyes, he sees through millions, and instead of touching and smiling and laughing and crying and welcoming and listening through two eyes and hands and ears, Jesus does so through one body composed of thousands and thousands of us. So one of the best things you can do for your friends who don't yet know and love Jesus is to introduce them to your other friends who do.

Jesus said that the love your unconvinced friends observe between you and your fellow disciples will be the most telling evidence possible for his legitimacy. They will sense his Spirit alive in you all, and—Paul put it this way (in 1 Corinthians 14)—they will fall down on their faces and say, "God is really among you!"

Of course, if your community of faith is riddled with arrogance, divided by pride, polluted with elitism, or stagnant with apathy, you have some preparatory work to do, namely, stirring up your community of faith so it can become what it was meant to be—a portal into the family of God.

In the context of imperfect but vibrant Christian community (even just two or three of you!), the message of Christ will come alive in a way that a disembodied booklet or lecture never could convey. And once your community begins to function as such a portal, a process will be set into motion that will not always be easy, but will be exciting and worthwhile because every new person who comes in will make your community even more ready to welcome the next.

4. The Journey Factor: See disciple-making as a holistic process and unending journey, not just a conversion event.

Let me repeat this: About two years passed between the first and last emails I shared with you in these pages. Two years! If you are surprised by how slow the process went, I am surprised at how fast it went. Alice covered a lot of ground in two years!

You will be more comfortable with the journey factor if you understand the difference between four kinds of thinking—boundary, centered, process, and journey thinking. Boundary thinking is always asking the same question: in or out? Christian or non-Christian? You could draw it like this:

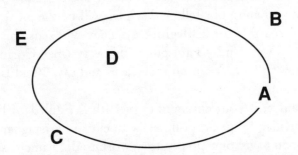

In this way of thinking, we are comfortable that D is in, and that E, B, and C are out. We are confused about A, who seems to be on the line. Centered thinking gets rid of the boundary, and instead focuses on a point we will call "X."

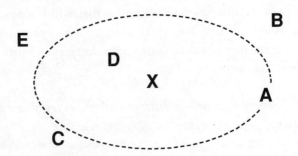

Now, as we de-emphasize "in/out," we become more aware of how close D is to the center, and we can make some interesting distinctions—such as that "outsider" C may be as close to the center as "almost insider" A is. But process thinking goes one step further.

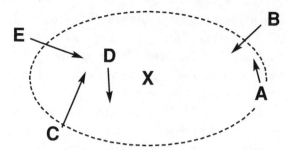

Now, let the arrows suggest direction and (by their length) speed or momentum, two factors that are invisible in the other ways of thinking. Now, it becomes clear that B and E are better off than A, even though they are "outsiders" by boundary thinking, and "distant" by centered thinking.

In process thinking, we are never content to simply pass judgment on someone's status (in or out) or location (near or far). Rather, we want to influence their direction and momentum as we are able.

For fun (and profit), we can torque the diagram once more, and talk about something beyond boundary, centered, and process thinking: journey thinking. In journey thinking, we realize that the center point isn't static. It is moving, progressing, advancing, and journeying. Now the most important question becomes whether one is following. Somehow, this should resonate with Jesus' primal call: follow me!

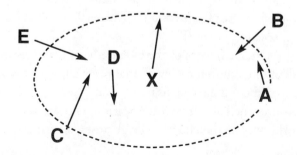

Now, who in this diagram would you rather to be—D or C, A or E? If "X" is Jesus, who is traveling with Jesus? Who has responded to the call of *follow me?* In the postmodern matrix, we cannot afford to limit ourselves to boundary thinking. Although there is certainly a place for boundaries, perhaps this diagram makes clear why we need other ways of thinking as well, more process-oriented and journey-oriented ways that will help us understand why Jesus would say "Many of the last will be first" and "Do not judge."

One of the negative effects of our boundary thinking has been this: What Jesus intended as a starting line became for us a finish line. Because of our boundary thinking, many of us got across the in/out barrier and parked there. But Jesus did not call us to a parking lot; he invited us on an adventure, an odyssey, a journey that will never end. Quite a difference!

5. The Holy Spirit Factor: Believe that God is at work "out there" in everyone (either working from the outside to get in or from the inside to get out), not just "in here" in the church.

Many people are experiencing the Holy Spirit but do not realize it. The Spirit of God reaches out to them through beauty, humor, joy, rest, excitement, justice, and mercy. In their sorrows, loneliness, guilt, and despair, they are being touched by God's Spirit too. In many ways, we simply come along to help them understand what already surrounds them, as Paul did at Mars Hill in Athens (see Acts 17:16 ff).

One of the tragic ironies of the twentieth century was the continual talk about "church renewal" that preoccupied us with how the Spirit would work through us in our church services. Meanwhile, Jesus was concerned about how the Spirit would work through us in the world outside the church—its ghettoes, art galleries, shops, schools, sidewalks, parks, fields, forests, apartment buildings, buses, trains, and office buildings. Maybe in the twenty-first century, we will have a better perspective about the Holy Spirit: He is trying either to get into the hearts of those who have not yet received him, or to get out of the hearts of those who have received him—get in to bless them, and get out to make them a blessing, expressing God's love and power and goodness and glory to everyone around.

The Holy Spirit factor reminds us that evangelism is not simply the transmission of information, it is a mysterious encounter between human beings (and human cultures and institutions too) and the Spirit of God, who loves, surrounds, and pursues them gently. It is our privilege to be part of that mysterious encounter.

6. The Learning Factor: See evangelism as part of your own discipleship—not just the other person's!

Like Peter with Cornelius, we all find that we learn lessons we never could have otherwise as we reach out with God's love. This learning posture helps protect us from the arrogance and brashness that were too common in our modern-era evangelism, as if we had found "it," figured it out, processed and packaged and sold it, but stopped learning from it ourselves.

7. The Missional Factor: See evangelism as recruiting people for God's mission on earth, not just people for heaven.

When Jesus says to go and make disciples, teaching the new disciples to do everything Jesus has taught, it is clear that Jesus is not just recruiting "souls" for heaven. He is sending his agents into the world. He is launching a revolution, which he called "the kingdom of God." Hatred and revenge will be replaced by love and mercy; lust and greed will be replaced by respect and generosity; hurry and stress will be replaced by joy and rest.

Thus every person whom we touch and influence through spiritual friendship will become one less person who is "part of the problem," and one more who is "part of the solution," using his or her time, talents, and treasure to help the world become the kind of place God desires it to be—more just, more compassionate, more beautiful, more safe, more exciting, more alive, more in line with Jesus' prayer: "Your kingdom come, your will be done on earth as it is in heaven." In this way, we contribute, one life at a time, to changing the world. This is not to say that questions of heaven and hell are unimportant. It is that they are not as exclusively important as modern Christians have tended to proclaim them to be. But this is another topic, for another book.

The fact is, our mission has two dimensions—a historic, here-and-now, down-to-earth dimension of changing lives, changing cultures, and changing history, and an eternal, ultimate, transcendent dimension of helping people become the kinds of people who will enjoy God forever beyond this life. Both were important to Jesus, and both must matter to us as well.

8. The Service Factor: See evangelism as one facet of our identity as servants to all.

As we have seen, my whole experience with Alice began with a simple act of service—helping her load her heavy and fragile harp into her vehicle. Should we be surprised that Jesus said our role in this earth is not one of critics, cynics, consumers, escapists, controllers, or isolationists—but rather servants? Jesus said he came not to be served, but to be a servant, and he demonstrated his service by washing the feet of his disciples, and then telling us that we should go and do likewise. "As the Father sent me, so I send you," he said. So the best first step for you as you finish this chapter would be to keep your eyes open—as a servant does, as a waiter does in a restaurant, simply looking for an opportunity to be of service.

It may start with a simple act of service, and lead down the road to someone discovering liberation from "this overwhelming disdain for everything inside of me," and in its place, feeling "a little of God's love." Like Alice, they will discover that they are "seeing it everywhere! In all these people's faces, in handshakes, in tears, in coincidences, in need. This spirit is so alive! . . . It's not discriminatory. It's pretty amazing."

Anyone can serve . . . anyone who is willing. And so, if you are willing, you are more ready than you realize.

19 | Feeling Like Your Heart Is Going to Explode

Look at those last sentences from Alice's email again:

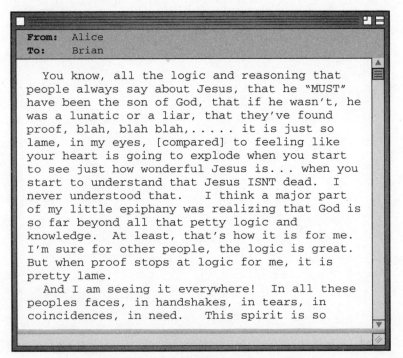

From: Alice
To: Brian

You know, all the logic and reasoning that people always say about Jesus, that he "MUST" have been the son of God, that if he wasn't, he was a lunatic or a liar, that they've found proof, blah, blah blah,..... it is just so lame, in my eyes, [compared] to feeling like your heart is going to explode when you start to see just how wonderful Jesus is... when you start to understand that Jesus ISNT dead. I never understood that. I think a major part of my little epiphany was realizing that God is so far beyond all that petty logic and knowledge. At least, that's how it is for me. I'm sure for other people, the logic is great. But when proof stops at logic for me, it is pretty lame.

And I am seeing it everywhere! In all these peoples faces, in handshakes, in tears, in coincidences, in need. This spirit is so

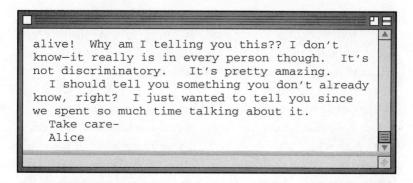

```
alive!  Why am I telling you this?? I don't
know—it really is in every person though.  It's
not discriminatory.   It's pretty amazing.
  I should tell you something you don't already
know, right?  I just wanted to tell you since
we spent so much time talking about it.
  Take care-
  Alice
```

Alice's comments about the lameness of logic bring me back to a speaking engagement a few years back. After the lecture, a young woman about Alice's age came up and thanked me for the talk. She paid me one of the most unusual, but on reflection one of the best, compliments I have ever received: "You are the first Christian pastor or minister I have ever heard who didn't act like Christianity owns God."

I find her statement fascinating. I see it closely related to the "blah, blah, blah" that has so turned off Alice. Let me slightly rephrase both young women: Modern Christianity has (inadvertently, I think) tended to reduce God to a being containable by human concepts or propositions or logic. It has too often acted as though it had God bottled, labeled, and hermetically sealed, a commodity we own and distribute at will, logically proven, and theologically defined. Too often, as Alice said, for us modern Christians "proof stops at logic."

This trend toward a domesticated God who is "owned" by Christianity is a recent (and I think blasphemous) development. No wonder evangelism seems dreary under these circumstances. As Walker Percy once wrote, instead of "Jesus saves!" we could as easily be shouting, "Exxon! Exxon!" because God has become a product that we are selling or promoting.

Christianity has not always been like this. Gregory of Nyssa of the fourth century once said, "Concepts create idols. Only wonder understands." Martin Luther reputedly reflected this realization: "If I could understand one grain of wheat, I would die of wonder." It is this kind of wonder that Alice expresses when she speaks of her heart exploding and her "little epiphany."

Only wonder understands. Jesus said the kingdom of God is like a man who plants seeds and then waits a while and then sees the seedlings rising to the sun and in the end, he "knows not how." It is a mystery and a wonder to him. Paul said the same thing: "One plants the seeds, another waters them, but only God can cause the growth" (1 Corinthians 3:5 ff).

That is why you have come nearly to the end of this book and you have not found any formulas or outlines or lists of Bible verses to memorize in a certain order to help you "share the gospel." This is not to say these things don't have value; I know many people who have been helped by them. But those things are modern contrivances, engineered to remove rather than convey wonder, and their usefulness may end with modernity. In the post-modern world, we may find ourselves returning to a situation more like that of the Bible itself where people come to faith in unique and non-formulaic ways, each one's path and story unlike those of any other. As C. S. Lewis once said, "Encore!" is the one prayer God doesn't seem to like to answer!

Do you realize this? Do you realize that Paul never shared "the Four Spiritual Laws," John never invited anyone to come forward and say a sinner's prayer so they could have a born-again experience, Peter never explained the four or five simple "steps to peace with God," St. Augustine never invited anyone to pray with him to receive Christ as personal Savior, Martin Luther never issued an altar call, Jesus himself never told anyone how to "become a

Christian"? (For starters, the term "Christian" wasn't even coined until years after Jesus' departure, and that moniker was created by outsiders, not by the followers of Christ themselves.)

So much of what we think of as evangelism is really a modern invention, much of it flowing from the revivalism of the American frontier in the 1800s. Those methods made perfect sense in their context. People generally knew the gospel; they had been raised in a culture saturated by it. Their refusal to follow, their indifference to the call of Christ, their indulgence in any number of sub-Christian behaviors were the result not of ignorance, but rather, rebellion. So no wonder the "evangelists" of those days would ride in on their horses and preach with high emotion and hot rhetoric! They were scolding recalcitrant children who knew better!

By the mid-1900s, the situation had changed. Then, it was less the hell-fire-and-brimstone rhetoric that reached the masses (although a sizable subculture of people had developed for whom this style of preaching became a kind of acquired taste, people who learned to enjoy talk of flames and torture—as hard as that may be to believe—and who learned to savor the technique ["Good sermon, pastor!"] of the preaching "performers"—perhaps not unlike the way people today appreciate professional wrestlers). By the 1960s, rather than hot rhetoric, more and more it was cool logic that seemed to win the day. And again, for a nation whose ethos most resembled that of engineers (one cohort even being called the "builder" generation) and whose lives had been formed by two world wars, it is no wonder that evangelism took shape in diagrams of bridges and engineer's steps and laws (like those of physics), and the language of "campaigns" (like military campaigns in World War II) and "crusades," so that apologetics was about amassing logical "ammunition" in the form of irrefutable arguments. Somehow, this language does not strike me as the sound of good news. In more recent years, we have moved from warfare imagery to more legal language, reflecting our litigious society, with the vocabulary of "cases" and "evidence" and "verdicts." A step forward, I'd say, but not, I hope, the final word.

So in the process of making our message clear, simple, compelling, and well-packaged (we might even say "canned"), I fear we squeezed out the wonder. This sad fact makes many of us wonder if we in some way squeezed out the gospel itself. Perhaps the best way for us to rediscover the gospel, wonder and all, is through the kind of spiritual friendship we have considered in this book!

Let me assure you that I learned all that "evangelism stuff"—the steps, the laws, the diagrams, the verses, the arguments, the responses to objections, the "answers" to questions. In many cases this approach has helped me. I could teach it to you. But I decided not to do so in this book for a number of reasons, which you by now can anticipate. First, it has already been done, and in some cases, done well. So rather than learning it all yourself, I would recommend you help your friends with certain kinds of questions by passing on a book that you have read and found helpful yourself (like C. S. Lewis's *Mere Christianity* [HarperCollins, 2001], Lee Strobel's *The Case for Christ* [Zondervan, 1998] or *The Case for Faith* [Zondervan, 2000], or my *Finding Faith* [Zondervan, 2000], which I hope is a bit more postmodern-friendly than many of the more modern apologetics). Second, when I have tried to train others in all the evangelism techniques, I have usually ended up intimidating rather than motivating my students. They leave saying, "Wow, you know a lot!" rather than "Wow, I can do this!"

Rather than overwhelming you, in this book I want to assure you, just as I tried to assure Alice, that you are already more ready than you realize. I can say that with confidence because almost anyone can be a friend.

There is one proviso: Far be it from me to say we should offer less than logic. Few of us are at risk of being too smart, too logical, too intelligent. Too many of us assume that "childlike faith" means ignorant faith, childish faith, stupid faith—another case of our amazing ability to miss the point. No, knowledge is good, wisdom is better, and logic is fine ... but proof needs to go, as Alice said, far beyond logic.

Gregory of Nyssa was right: Concepts become idols. Only wonder understands. This is why I believe that in the end, the most important thing you can communicate to anyone is something beyond your logic and arguments—your own humbled sense of wonder, passion, and love—the very things that canned formulas have a way of squeezing out.

What do I mean by wonder? I can't do better than Alice's own words:

> ... feeling like your heart is going to explode when you start to see just how wonderful Jesus is... when you start to understand that Jesus ISNT dead. I never understood that. I think a major part of my little epiphany was realizing that God is so far beyond all that petty logic and knowledge. At least, that's how it is for me. I'm sure for other people, the logic is great. But when proof stops at logic for me, it is pretty lame.
>
> And I am seeing it everywhere! In all these peoples faces, in handshakes, in tears, in coincidences, in need. This spirit is so alive! Why am I telling you this?? I don't know—it really is in every person though. It's not discriminatory. It's pretty amazing.

The more that I know, the more that I learn, the more wonder I feel about how wonderful ("pretty amazing!" in Alice's delicious understatement) God the Father is, how wonderful Jesus is, how wonderful the Holy Spirit is, how wonderful the gospel is, how wonderful life is! The whole Christian message becomes for me less an outline of information and more a wonderful song. It is less a thesis to be argued and proved and more a mystery to celebrate and sing and dance. I think of a beautiful medieval poem celebrating the incarnation and birth of Christ, an anonymous work that has been set to music by many composers (perhaps most powerfully by Morten Lauridsen), which I'll quote below in both Latin and English:

> O magnum mysterium, (O great mystery)
> Et admirabile sacramentum, (and wondrous sacrament)
> Ut animalia viderent Dominum naturm (that animals should see the newborn Lord)
> Jacentem in praesepio! (lying in a manger!)
> Beata virgo, cujus viscera meruerent, (Blessed is the virgin whose womb was worthy)
> Portare dominum Christum. Alleluia! (to bear our Lord Christ. Alleluia!)
> Domine, audivi auditum tuum et timui; (Lord, I heard your call and was afraid;)
> Consideravi opera tua (I considered your works)
> Et expavi in medio duorum animalium. (and I trembled between two animals.)

This poem reminds me that whenever we converse about God, we must remember that we are just little human beings trembling between an ox and an ass, beholding mysteries too wonderful for words, too wonderful for minds, so wonderful that they threaten to make our hearts explode with wonder. The wonder is so great that all our conversations about God must be touched with humility, maybe even a certain sadness (in recognition of how far short our best words fall—remember the philosopher petting his golden retriever?), but yet with joy that we little humans can speak of the Wonder at all!

And so, we dance. We dance in service, in gratitude, in hard work well done, in prayer, in game, in tilling the soil and crafting the poem, in hiking and sailing and flying, in hanging out, in sharing a drink of coffee or beer or wine or cold water, in joy, in sorrow, in hope, in disappointment. We dance. Sometimes we dance with our eyes closed, dizzy, spinning, with tears streaming down our faces. Sometimes we dance with such joy that we feel like our hearts are going to explode!

And when we open our eyes, we see that we do not dance alone, but that others have joined us, and the dance we share is beautiful, because the music that moves us resounds with the holiest mystery of all. So shall we dance?

20 | A Whole New Category of Humanity

My friend Todd had one of those "punctiliar conversions"—a datable, definable night when he became a follower of Christ, a clear turning point, a life-changing "born again" experience. After hearing an evangelist communicate the good news and call for a commitment, Todd responded and knew that his life would never be the same. The evangelist gave out some literature after the meeting, and Todd came home and devoured it.

Like a lot of "follow-up" literature from the 1970s, it included Bible verses to look up on your own, which Todd did, but there was a problem. Being unfamiliar with the Bible, he didn't really understand the "verse system" used by the literature. When it said to read "2 Corinthians 5:17," Todd didn't realize you were supposed to stop reading when you came to verse 18. So, although the pamphlet intended for him to read only this:

> 17Therefore, if anyone is in Christ, he is a new creation; the old has gone, the new has come!

Todd naïvely (but wisely) read all of this:

> 17Therefore, if anyone is in Christ, he is a new creation; the old has gone, the new has come! 18All this is from God, who reconciled us to himself through Christ and

gave us the ministry of reconciliation: [19]that God was rec-
onciling the world to himself in Christ, not counting
men's sins against them. And he has committed to us the
message of reconciliation. [20]We are therefore Christ's
ambassadors, as though God were making his appeal
through us. We implore you on Christ's behalf: Be reconciled to God.

Something profound struck Todd that first night of his life as a
Christian, something that many Christians, probably even many
pastors, don't consider. As he read the phrase, "new creation," he
naturally wondered, "What does that mean?" And because he was
too naïve to stop at the end of verse 17, he kept reading and found
the answer in verse 20: We are *Christ's ambassadors*. In other
words, Paul says, "If anyone is in Christ, he is something completely new—a new kind of creature on earth—namely, an ambassador of Christ, a peace ambassador inviting people to be
reconciled to God."

Because Todd got this straight his very first night as a Christian, his spiritual life took a different trajectory than that of many
new converts. Looking back, I think something similar happened
to me. I went through a crisis of faith in my early teenage years
that led to a wholehearted Christian commitment. The first thing
I did was start a Bible study at my school, but the thought of inviting Christians to the study never crossed my mind. After all,
Christians already "get it," so why invite them? Instead, I invited
three friends who weren't Christians at all. From the start, to me,
to be a Christian meant to be a peace agent of Christ, an ambassador to the irreligious (and the religious too, I suppose). Being
reconciled to God meant helping others be reconciled too.

When I don't stop reading at verse 17, I realize that in Paul's
mind, there were two kinds of "old creations" in the world. First,

there were the irreligious. Nothing particularly new there—selfishness, materialism, lust, greed, arrogance, apathy, prejudice, ungratefulness, conflict. Second, there were the religious—again, pretty predictable, pretty standard: rituals, rules, piety, worship, meetings, learning, prayers, isolation. But in Christ, God wasn't just creating more religious people; instead, God was forming a new kind of person, a whole new category of humanity. Unlike the irreligious, these people loved God. But unlike the religious, they loved the irreligious! Not only did they love them, but they understood their own whole identity as being sent on a mission to the irreligious, a peace mission, as agents of Christ. In other words, before this you could say there were two categories of humanity: the sick and the healthy. Now there was a third: the healers.

The mission of the peace agents or healers was not a matter of condemnation, judgment, or scolding—again, the standard postures of the religious. Rather, the new kind of people created in Christ are healing ministers of reconciliation, sent out with good news to the irreligious: God is not holding their sins against them because Jesus somehow achieved a kind of reversal, where he suffered for our sins and passed on his goodness to us. Now we are reconciled to God, righteous in God's eyes with "the righteousness of Christ."

These people of this new category have themselves accepted this gift of reconciliation, and with it, they have accepted the call to become agents of reconciliation—peace ambassadors, people through whom God's plea—"Be reconciled to God!"—is heard. (By the way, notice how this dynamic balance—reconciled, to become agents of reconciliation—perfectly mirrors the ancient calling of Abraham—blessed, to be a blessing to the world.)

Again, Todd understood this element of Christian identity from the first night of his Christian life, and somehow, I think I did too, from the first months of my discipleship. But maybe you have not (until now?) understood this. Maybe for you, evangelism (or spiritual friendship, or disciple-making, or whatever you want to call it) has been a kind of optional add-on, like electric door locks or a CD player in a car. This is sad, I think, and wrong, but that's okay. It is not too late to get a fresh understanding, and it is not too late for a new beginning!

The fact is, too many (maybe even most) Christians probably stop reading after verse 17. For them, "new creation" just means "being reconciled to God," or "having a new status before God," or "going to heaven" or "being blessed" or "being forgiven." They do not realize that the whole idea of being "in Christ" is being in his mission of reconciliation as well as being reconciled, being a blessing as well as being blessed. And again, this is sad, I think, and wrong, but it is not too late for a change.

If enough Christians, like Todd, start forgetting to stop reading at verse 17, if they stop chopping up the Bible into little parcels like that so that they miss the bigger picture, then I think we can expect a revolution, a new day in the church. Because Christians who understand their identity as Christ's peace ambassadors or agents of reconciliation will revolutionize the church. And churches revolutionized in this way will in turn revolutionize the world, which is what I am living for, and the reason I wrote this book.

So where do we go from here? Good books make you want to put them down and go do something. They make you want to stop reading and start living. I hope this is the case here. Here are a few ideas:

1. If you are interested in more study and reflection, I have included two resources in the appendix: a study I call "Disciple!" and a list of Bible passages and other resources for

further consideration. You may want to use these in a small group study, or meet with a friend and go through them together, sharing your insights. But don't stop there!

2. Even more important, keep your eyes open. There might be someone struggling to load something (like a two-year-old!) into a minivan and you could help. Or there may be a colleague who could join you for lunch, or a neighbor who's up for a game of basketball, and if you befriend these people, sharing some of your precious time with them, a true spiritual friendship could develop over time, with many wonderful and intriguing conversations leading to some life-changing realizations and changes in direction—for both of you! And as for answers to their questions and that sort of thing, you don't have to have it all figured out in advance, because the friendship would be about you learning right along with your friend.

You see, you are more ready than you realize!

Here's my benediction for you:

> *O God, we love you and we love people, and our love is a response to that love with which you first loved us. Thank you for apprehending us mercifully through Jesus Christ, and calling us from trivial pursuits and destructive ways to this high and holy calling of spiritual friendship, so that through us, your good news can flow to others, and together, we can join the dance that never ends. Send us into our world to spread, through our words and deeds, the Word of your wonder. May the dance go on! Amen!*

Afterword

Many of the names and some details in the stories in this book have been changed in respect for people's privacy. Please be assured though that these stories emerge from real-life, down-to-earth, day-to-day experiences.

Not all (and perhaps, not even *most*) real-life stories have endings as "happy" as those I have shared in this book. As Jesus said (in Matthew 13), the number of seeds we sow far exceeds the number of "happy endings" we see. A book full of stories with happy endings could give the opposite impression, and stories intended to encourage could thus actually discourage over the long run by inflating our expectations beyond what is realistic.

The fact is, I have engaged in many spiritual friendships that have resolved into ambiguity or misunderstanding, not joy or convergence. And many times—far more than I'm aware of—I haven't said "just the right thing," but rather, have unintentionally hurt or confused people. Too often, I'm sure, like the crowd in the story of Zaccheus (Luke 19), I have gotten in the way, and if God has touched others around me, it has been *in spite of* me, not *through* me.

With this realism in mind, I recall some wise words from trappist monk Thomas Merton (which I came across in Jim Wallis' wonderful book, *Faith Works: Lessons from the Life of an Activist Preacher*, Random House, 2000). Shortly before Merton's untimely death, he wrote a letter to a friend, a social activist named

Jim Forrest. What Merton said regarding social activism is also true of the subject we have considered in these pages.

"Do not depend on the hope of results," Merton said. Being involved in God's work requires us to face the fact that our work will at times appear to achieve ... "no result at all, if not perhaps results opposite to what you expect." Far better than being obsessed with results, then, whether in social work or evangelism, is to focus on the value of the work itself, and on the value of being genuine friends with those we serve.

This emphasis on friendship keeps us from turning evangelism into just another set of slogans and causes. Because slogans and causes don't sustain, the monk warned: "... in the end one is left holding the bag, empty, with no trace of meaning left in it. And then the temptation is to yell louder than ever in order to make the meaning be there again by magic...."

Merton also warned his friend from using his social work to make an identity for himself. Similarly, we can try to use our evangelistic work to protect ourselves against "nothingness, annihilation." We can try to *be* somebody by being an *evangelist*, which is pretty pathetic. Merton has it right: "All the good that you will do will come not from you but from the fact that you have allowed yourself, in the obedience of faith, to be used by God's love." With this in mind, we can stop trying to prove ourselves, and instead be channels of God's power, which can work through us without our even realizing it, Merton affirms.

So neither a dependence upon results nor loyalty to a cause nor the need to build an identity for ourselves can motivate us and sustain us over the long run. Rather, he advised, "If you can get free from the domination of causes and just serve Christ's truth, you will be able to do more and will be less crushed by the inevitable disappointments."

Acknowledging the reality of "much disappointment, frustration, and confusion," Merton concludes, our hope is "... not in something we think we can do but in God who is making something good out of it in some way we cannot see."

This book was in its final editing stages when our world was rocked by the events of September 11, 2001. At this moment as I write, everyone is filled with uncertainty and anxiety. Amidst all of this uncertainty, and acknowledging life's inevitable "disappointment, frustration and confusion," I think you will share my conviction that the world needs bearers/carriers/messengers/examples of the love of God now even more poignantly than ever. As Merton said, "The real hope ... is not in something we think we can do but in God...."

Appendix 1:
A Bible Study on Disciple-Making

If we engage in spiritual friendship, if we see evangelism as relational dance rather than conceptual conquest, process rather than event, mutual learning rather than sales pitch, I believe we will find our whole understanding of what it means to be a Christian will begin to change. Changing this one element will eventually change the whole system. For example, imagine a spider web from which a section of the web has been knocked out by a storm (or a big dragonfly), leaving it to sag dangerously. Then you watch the spider begin to rebuild or restring the deconstructed section, strand by strand. As she rebuilds and retightens the elements of the web, the whole web will feel the realignment. The web will be good as new—maybe even better—but nothing will be exactly the same as before.

Like Peter befriending Cornelius, as we seek to help others come to Christ, we will come to Christ in new ways ourselves. I would like to imagine that because you are engaging in this new approach to evangelism, your whole system is being deconstructed and reconstructed, realigned, recalibrated strand by strand. I would like to propose a new way of thinking about being a Christian that results from this new emphasis on and understanding of evangelism.

However, as ironic as it might sound in a book with "evangelism" in its title, I believe *evangelism* may be a less and less useful term in the future. I find myself replacing it more and more with the term *disciple-making*. Let me explain.

I have noticed a progression going on. In a paradigm that is event-focused, we have evangelism and follow-up. (If we become more sophisticated, we add pre-evangelism to the front side of the equation.) Then, when we begin to feel that "follow-up" is a rather thin description of spiritual growth, we speak of evangelism and discipleship, or evangelism and spiritual formation. But then, when we see the dynamic, holistic, and relational process overshadowing the single conversion event so that the event only has meaning for us within the larger process, we find ourselves speaking more and more in terms of disciple-making. And at that moment, something wonderful happens: We find ourselves transported out from our stuffy classrooms and air-conditioned church halls, our meetings and committees and liturgies and Bible studies. And we find ourselves touching down, blinking and wide-eyed, inside the wild world of gospel stories with Jesus and his original disciples—wind in our hair, sea spray in our faces, the smell of fish cooking over glowing embers on the beach, the cries of sea gulls, the laughter of children, the music of wedding banquets, and the sound of his voice, saying, "Once there was a man who had two sons..."

The world desperately needs this fresh emphasis on a holistic disciple-making process over an isolated conversion event, according to my friend and noted missiologist Jim Engel:

> There is widespread agreement that the western-driven agenda of the last 50 years to "finish the task" of world evangelization has tragically missed the mark in its narrow focus only on conversion. As I have often said, the

Great Commission has become a "great commotion" of proclamation in virtual disregard of spiritual formation (doing the business of making disciples) and social transformation (righteousness and justice). (*Development Associates International,* vol. 4, no. 2 [August 2001]: p. 5)

What is disciple-making? In a sentence, it is being a disciple and helping others become disciples too, as part of the ongoing movement of spiritual friendship begun by Jesus Christ. But this definition requires us to think more deeply about what "disciple" means. To do that, I would like to offer a seven-lesson study on the word "disciple" that I originally prepared for people in my church. If you are a relative newcomer to the Christian faith, I hope this will serve as a good orientation to discipleship for you, and if you are a longstanding Christian veteran, perhaps this study (if you can approach it with fresh eyes and an open heart) can be for you a needed reorientation, a reconstruction of your web of belief. From that new vantage point, the dance of evangelism will make more sense, I believe. (By the way, a version of this study is available online at our church website, *www.crcc.org,* if you want to recommend it to a friend.)

In my speaking and writing, I generally try to avoid using religious jargon. I believe that God's message is best understood when expressed in common words, in down-to-earth vocabulary. (That is how Jesus talked—in plain language, telling real-life stories, making simple but profound comparisons to familiar things.) Sometimes, however, a "religious" word is too rich in meaning to be translated into a more familiar term, which is the case with the word "disciple." In modern culture, there is not a satisfactory synonym ... although a constellation of near-synonyms like student, learner, apprentice, follower, agent, and protégé together are better than any one word alone.

It is best to go back to the Gospels themselves to get an idea of what a disciple is. So let's go to the last few sentences in the Gospel of Matthew, one of the four accounts of Jesus' life. At this point in the story, Jesus has been crucified and has risen from the grave. He has appeared to his disciples and told them to meet him about sixty miles north of Jerusalem.

> Then the eleven disciples went to Galilee, to the mountain where Jesus had told them to go. When they saw him, they worshiped him, but some doubted. Then Jesus came to them and said, "All authority in heaven and on earth has been given to me. Therefore go and make disciples of all nations, baptizing them in the name of the Father and of the Son and of the Holy Spirit, and teaching them to obey everything I have commanded you. And surely I am with you always, to the very end of the age." (Matthew 28:16–20)

These words will be the focal point of our whole seven-part study, so before we go on, let me encourage you to reread the passage, and ask yourself a few questions. What one word or thought in the passage makes the biggest impression on you? Why? What additional questions does this passage raise in your mind? If you had been one of the Eleven, what would you have been thinking or feeling as you heard these words? Let's try to get a fresh vision of evangelism as disciple-making by rebuilding our understanding of what *disciple* means.

Lesson 1: Disciples Are People Who Have Confidence in Jesus

The words "all authority ... has been given to me" tell us that disciples are people who have confidence in the full authority of Jesus.

What does it mean to believe that Jesus has full authority? I'd suggest three things:

1. It means you believe that Jesus is alive. That's significant!

2. It means you believe that Jesus is right about everything. You believe that what he taught was true—and that God affirmed that Jesus was right by raising him from the dead.

3. It means you believe that what Jesus said about himself was true—that he was indeed sent from God, that he was and is the Son of God, and that he is in fact the Savior of the world.

Now you may be put off by the word "believe." You may be thinking, "But I'm not certain!" Look at the passage again: "When they saw him, they worshiped him, but some doubted." That sentence tells us at least two important things:

1. When you have confidence in Jesus' full authority, you worship him. You believe that he fully and accurately reflects God's own glory, and that amazing belief unleashes in you a song and a celebration.

2. Even Jesus' disciples sometimes have doubts. Having doubts does not disqualify you as a disciple at all. In fact, having doubts qualifies you as being a living human being whose mind is engaged and whose heart is curious, a state of being that Jesus encourages wherever he goes! So disciples doubt sometimes, but as a disciple, you do not let your doubts control your life. You have doubts, but you don't let your doubts have you.

Having confidence in Jesus' authority is essential for discipleship. How much confidence do you need? I'd say, "Enough to get moving and follow him." If you don't trust Jesus is on the right track, why follow him? If you don't believe he speaks God's truth, why learn from him? If you aren't convinced he uniquely represents, embodies, and "radiates" God, why pattern your life after him? If you don't think he is and has what the world needs, why be an agent of his agenda for changing the world?

But if you are convinced, why not follow him with your whole heart (belief and doubts, hopes and fears) and learn all he wants to teach you, joining him in his mission?

There is a counterpart to our confidence in Jesus; it is a quality that must exist in us. We might call it "teachability." It is the humility to admit that you do not already know all the answers, you have a lot to learn, you are wrong about more things than you realize, and it is the curiosity, hunger, thirst, and urge to seek and find and seek some more. Disciples by definition are learners, not know-it-alls. If you ever start acting like a know-it-all, you have stopped being a real disciple. To be a disciple means to have so much confidence in Jesus that you become his lifelong student, a learner for life.

Let's do a little self-assessment and response.

Do you have confidence in the full authority of Jesus? This is different from having confidence in the church or Christianity. Discipleship requires first and foremost confidence in Jesus, not anybody or anything else. It is not *complete confidence* in the authority of Jesus, but rather *confidence* in the full authority of Jesus. We are acknowledging that even disciples do not have complete confidence at times. Your confidence, after all, isn't in your confidence; it is in Jesus. Do you see the difference?

Do you believe he is alive? Even though you can't see him or touch him, do you believe Jesus is in some way with you, with us, with the world, so we are not just talking about some dead guy's ideas, but rather a living person's presence and mission?

Do you believe he is right in everything he taught? This does not mean you understand everything he taught, but that you are biased to give the benefit of the doubt to him.

Do you believe he is who he claimed to be—the Savior of the world, the Son of God, your Savior?

Take a minute and talk to Jesus now, and affirm to him what you believe about him.

Lesson 1 Review

Disciples have confidence in the full authority of Jesus. They believe he is alive, that he is right in everything he taught, that he is who he claimed to be.

Lesson 2: Disciples Are People Who Have a Mission

Read the passage again....

> Then the eleven disciples went to Galilee, to the mountain where Jesus had told them to go. When they saw him, they worshiped him, but some doubted. Then Jesus came to them and said, "All authority in heaven and on earth has been given to me. Therefore **go and make disciples** of all nations, baptizing them in the name of the Father and of the Son and of the Holy Spirit, and teaching them to obey everything I have commanded you. And surely I am with you always, to the very end of the age." (Matthew 28:16–20)

The simple word *go* tells us that disciples are people who have been sent on a mission.

When the text says "go," the actual grammatical construction (in the original Greek text) says "as you are going," or "as you go." The idea is, "Wherever you go, wherever your journey takes you. . . ." Since your work will involve "all nations," you realize that Jesus' disciples will be going a long way from home!

To be a disciple means you have confidence in Jesus' authority, so when he says you will be "on the go," you understand your life will be a journey, an adventure, a mission. But what is the mission?

The obvious answer is "make disciples." But that answer implies that you must first be a disciple yourself. (You can't help someone else become what you are not yourself exemplifying, right?) So, let's define our mission like this:

To be disciples...
And to make disciples.

In other words, Jesus sends us into the world to learn to live life to the full as he taught, and to help others learn to live life to the full as he taught too. Our mission is about being and making disciples.

When Jesus says, "teaching them to obey everything I have commanded you," he is putting the two sides of the coin together.

I have commanded you—being disciples
Teaching them—making disciples

In modern times, we have often missed how powerful these words are. Jesus does not say, "Teach them the information I have informed you with" or, "Teach them the belief system I have taught you." Rather, he says, "I have taught you a way of life, a way to *do life.* Practice that way of life. Do life as I have taught you, and teach others to live as you have begun learning to live. Teach others all over the world the way of life you have learned from me."

There is a powerful balance in these words: *Teaching them to obey everything I have commanded you.* Some people reduce being a disciple to quietly obeying in their private lives without teaching others, and some focus on teaching without exemplifying. But it is clear that to be a disciple means to learn to live Jesus' message ... and to influence others to do the same.

It is time for a personal assessment.

Have you accepted this as your mission—to be a disciple and make disciples, to learn to live as Jesus teaches, and to help others to do so as well?

Think of all the competing missions people live by—

to acquire wealth or possessions
to achieve comfort or enjoy leisure
to be popular or powerful or famous
to gain personal security or live quietly with one's family
to advance a political cause

Are you willing to put this mission from Jesus Christ above all others in your one and only life?

Discipleship doesn't just face you with a question about your belief system. It faces you with the challenge of a mission—a mission that you will accept or reject, a mission that you will give priority to, or a mission that you will subordinate to other priorities.

Before we move on, take a few minutes to write a prayer that expresses to God your response to Jesus' call to mission. You could begin by saying, "God, I accept this mission..."

Lesson 2 Review

Disciples are people with a mission: to be and make disciples.

Lesson 3: Disciples Are Identified As Disciples

Jesus said, "Therefore go and make disciples of all nations, **baptizing** them in the name of the Father and of the Son and of the Holy Spirit..."

What does "baptizing" mean?

Let's define it two ways: Baptism is a ritual or practice involving water to identify someone as a disciple of Jesus. Baptizing is identifying someone as a disciple of Jesus through a ritual or practice using water.

Unfortunately, it is easy to get distracted by a lot of theological controversies when the subject of baptism comes up. Let's not get distracted by the mode of baptism (should we immerse, pour, or sprinkle the water?) or the timing of baptism (should infants be baptized in anticipation of their eventual commitment to become disciples—or as an expression of their parents' commitment to raise them as disciples? Or should only people be baptized who are old enough to make their own meaningful commitment?). Rather let's focus on the meaning of baptism.

Baptism is rich in meaning. It suggests cleansing. When you are a disciple, you understand that you are cleansed by Christ. You understand that Christ died in your place on the cross, paying for your sins, fully forgiving you for all your wrongs. You are cleansed from guilt, and you are becoming a cleaner, healthier, more whole person.

Baptism suggests an ending and a new beginning. Immersion especially dramatizes this: a person is buried under the water—signifying the end of his or her old "BC" (before Christ) life—and then rises up out of the water—signifying the beginning of his or her new life as a disciple.

Baptism indicates a new identity. Here's an analogy: When a woman gets married, she accepts and wears a ring, which is a symbol of her vow and commitment. The ring isn't what makes her married, and it isn't what makes her love her husband. The commitment is what makes her married, and the relationship is what makes her love her husband. But she wears the ring as a symbol of her new identity as a woman in commitment and relationship to her new husband.

Baptism suggests that a person has similarly entered into a relationship with and commitment to Jesus Christ. It says, "Our relationship has progressed from a casual acquaintance or friendship to a deep, lifelong commitment." Not only that, but through baptism, like wearing a wedding ring, a person is going public. She is saying, "I'm not ashamed of this commitment. I want to be publicly identified as a person of commitment, a person in lifelong relationship to someone I love and who loves me."

In a marriage, the ring is often associated with taking on a new name, which suggests a new identity. A woman says, "I am now the wife of John," or a man says, "I am now the husband of Joan." Before those words were not true; now they are. Now they describe a new identity, which is why the words in bold below are so important:

> All authority in heaven and on earth has been given to me. Therefore go and make disciples of all nations, **baptizing them in the name of the Father and of the Son and of the Holy Spirit.**

Baptism means that you now identify God as your Father, Jesus as God's Son, and the Holy Spirit as God not only "up there" or "out there" but also God "in here"—God alive and present in your own heart, your own life. It means you are not ashamed of this new identity. It means you are going public with your commitment.

If you are committed to learn from Jesus how to live life to the full, if you are committed to help others learn to live that way too, if you have accepted God's invitation into a lifelong relationship, if you have accepted this new identity as a disciple, then you should be baptized to demonstrate that commitment. By being baptized, you will be saying, "I am a disciple, and I am committed to the mission of helping others become disciples too." As you help others become disciples, you'll invite them to "go public" in this way too.

Lesson 3 Review

Disciples are identified as disciples.

Lesson 4: Disciples Learn and Teach

Take a look at our passage again:

> Then the eleven disciples went to Galilee, to the mountain where Jesus had told them to go. When they saw him, they worshiped him, but some doubted. Then Jesus came to them and said, "All authority in heaven and on earth has been given to me. Therefore **go and make disciples** of all nations, baptizing them in the name of the Father and of the Son and of the Holy Spirit, and **teaching them** to obey everything I have commanded you. And surely I am with you always, to the very end of the age." (Matthew 28:16–20)

When Jesus chose his original disciples, we are told that they were chosen for two reasons: "to be with him" and "to be sent out."

The "to be with him" focuses on the disciple as learner. The "to be sent out" focuses on the disciple as teacher. Obviously, the two need to go together.

You may not think of yourself as a teacher. But you must remember that teaching isn't just lecturing in front of a bunch of bored people in rows of desks! Teaching happens in many ways.

Most important, we teach by example. Jesus modeled a way of life for us, and we learn it and model it for others. That's what brought Christ's message down through the centuries—teaching by example, passed down from generation to generation.

In what areas of your life are you a good and growing (nobody expects you to be faultless) example? What areas of your life do not yet set a good example?

Example is essential, but it is not the only essential dimension of our mission as disciples. How do we put our faith into words to help other people?

Jesus' example in this teaches us so much. Jesus used simple and clear language. He told stories—lots of stories. He made comparisons to familiar things. And he engaged in dialogue with people—he asked questions and listened; he never just talked at people.

For you to teach others, here are four suggestions:

1. Listen to their story. Cultivate a simple and wholehearted fascination with people. Show respect for them by being interested in their lives, interests, backgrounds. Ask lots of questions. If you feel it is appropriate to talk about spiritual matters, ask a question like, "Do you have a religious background?" Or invite them to talk by saying, "Tell me about your spiritual background." Sometimes, just asking, "Do you believe in God?" or "Where are you spiritually?" can open the door for great conversations. God has been at work in their lives long before you came on the scene, so respect God's previous involvement in their story by learning about it.

2. Tell them your story. It is often best to be very gentle in this by asking permission or opening the door for further conversation, saying something like, "Sometime, if you're interested, I can tell you about my own spiritual journey." Or

you can engage their curiosity by saying, "A few years ago, my life took a big turn for the better. I started paying more attention to the spiritual side of life." Or share with them what's going on in your life these days: "I heard a really good message at church yesterday...."

3. Tell them God's story. There's nothing better than simply recounting some of the stories from the Bible, especially stories by and about Jesus. I often find myself saying, at various points in a spiritual conversation, "That reminds me of a story Jesus told," or "That reminds me of a story about Jesus."

4. Be an inviter, bringer, and includer. If your friend is interested in learning more, invite him or her to church, or bring your friend into a circle of friends who share your faith. Include your as-yet-uncommitted friends in your life, so they can see your faith lived out in your personal life and the lives of your fellow disciples.

Remember that your mission is not just to convey information. Your mission is to teach people a new way of living. You are not just teaching them about dancing; you are helping them learn to dance.

Let's pause for a moment. Think of a few friends of yours who could benefit by learning more about following Jesus from you. Write down their names. Pray for them. Plan to spend some time with them. See if "teachable moments" occur when you can dialogue with them about things that truly matter.

Lesson 4 Review

Disciples teach.

Lesson 5: Disciples Have a Global/Local Vision

Notice the words in bold below:

> Therefore go and make disciples **of all nations**, baptizing them in the name of the Father and of the Son and of the Holy Spirit, and teaching them to obey all I have commanded you.

Those three words may not shock us, but they must have shocked the original disciples. Why?

Jesus and all the original disciples were Jewish. Most Jewish people in those days assumed that they alone had the treasure of knowing the one true and living God. To say "make disciples of all nations" would have been a staggering change in perspective for them.

Really, Jesus had been stretching their thinking in this direction all along. He reached out to all kinds of outsiders and outcasts—prostitutes, tax collectors, etc. It was clear that to Jesus, God's love extended much farther than most religious people of his day realized.

So in the words "of all nations," Jesus is telling us that we have a global mission and a global vision. We are an expression of God's love for the whole world.

It helps to get the big story in view. The story begins with creation—God creates a good and beautiful universe, including our planet, including life, including human beings. Humans are given a special responsibility to care for the planet, and to live in relationship with God. However, we have disregarded that special responsibility and rejected that relationship with God. The result? Violence, oppression, injustice, shame, and suffering.

God's remedy for the situation was to call one group of people into a special relationship with God. God's desire was to rescue and bless everyone in the world, and so he called one group of people to become his agents to bring blessing to everyone else. We see this global desire in God's words to Abraham, the father of the Jewish people, back in the book of Genesis: "I will bless you and make you a blessing. . . . Through you, all the nations of the world will be blessed."

Do you see the connection between "make disciples of all nations" and "all the nations of the world will be blessed"?

Of course, if you have a vision of changing the world, you have to work that global vision out locally, which is the purpose of churches. Churches are the places where disciples work on their global vision locally.

It is important to remember that God's goal isn't to bless the church only. His goal, through the church, is to bless the world. We exist for God's purpose that goes beyond ourselves. It is not "all about me" or even "all about us." Imagine how the world would become a better place if more and more people learned to live as Jesus taught—loving their neighbors as themselves, learning to forgive, discovering the joy of serving others, seeking God's kingdom first.

"All the nations" means that true disciples learn to love and respect all cultures. It means they are unalterably opposed to racism and prejudice. It means that they show special concern for those who are most likely to be forgotten—the poor, the sick, the elderly, the minority, the disabled.

Our global concern does not mean that we impose our culture on other people. It means that we seek to help people of all cultures to learn to live life to the full as Jesus wants them to do so in their culture. Jesus doesn't come to drive out the culture of a people and replace it with an alien one. He comes to drive out the evil from their culture so it can become even more beautiful, alive, unique, wonderful, and good.

It is a global mission, but it must be worked out locally. If you have this understanding, you will not see the church as a purveyor of religious goods and services, which you attend as a consumer. Instead, you will see the church as a community of people engaged in mission, and you will see yourself as a partner in that mission, using your time, talent, and treasure in alignment with God's purposes, in teamwork with others.

Your time: You will give priority to gathering with your fellow disciples for worship, teaching, fellowship, prayer, and service. In our over-busy world, this is not easy, but it is something disciples do. They build a rhythm of life not around work, work, work (or play, play, play), but around work and rest, worship and service, fellowship and teaching, praying and playing.

Your talent: You will discover and use your special God-given gifts and abilities to help the church in its mission. You may have a special gift in leadership, in helping needy people, in administration, in teaching, in hospitality, in encouraging others. Whatever your gift, you will use it wholeheartedly, in a spirit of love.

Your treasure: You will take a portion of all your income and invest it in the mission of your church. What percentage of income is appropriate? In the Bible, ten percent is the consistent benchmark, but it certainly should not be considered a ceiling. Really, we understand that everything we have and earn is a gift from God, so it all ultimately belongs to him.

The vision is local—but it is also global. That means we are all "on-call" and may receive "orders" to go anywhere to be and make disciples. Wherever we are, we seek to work that global vision out locally through the missional community of the church. We are to be missional people, in missional churches, with a vision for the whole world.

Here are some questions for you to consider:

Have you ever told God you are willing to go wherever he calls you to go?

Are there any traces of prejudice in your life?

Do you believe that God loves all people, all nations, everyone in the world?

Do you see yourself as a consumer and the church as a provider of religious goods and services—or do you see yourself as a partner in the church, which is a community engaged in God's mission?

Are you investing your time in God's global and local missions? When, where, and how?

Are you investing your talent in God's global and local missions? What mix of talents do you uniquely bring?

Are you investing your treasure in God's global and local missions? What percentage of your income expresses your commitment?

Lesson 5 Review

Disciples have global and local visions.

Lesson 6: Disciples Are Empowered

Consider again the last, climactic words of Matthew's Gospel, paying special attention to how they crescendo at the last sentence:

Then the eleven disciples went to Galilee, to the mountain where Jesus had told them to go. When they saw him, they worshiped him, but some doubted. Then Jesus came to them and said, "All authority in heaven and on earth

has been given to me. Therefore go and make disciples of
all nations, baptizing them in the name of the Father and
of the Son and of the Holy Spirit, and teaching them to
obey everything I have commanded you. And surely **I am
with you always,** to the very end of the age." (Matthew
28:16–20)

Ironically, Jesus spoke those words just before disappearing
from their sight. Why would he say, "I am with you always" as
he was apparently leaving them?

Some days before, Jesus had explained that he was going away,
but would send his Spirit to be with the disciples, and not only
with them, but also in them.

His Spirit would do many things for them: teach them, guide
them, encourage them, unify them, make them aware when they
had done wrong, assure them they were God's beloved children,
activate special spiritual gifts in them, give them boldness, transform them into increasingly Christ-like people, energize them,
and empower them.

It is essential for disciples to believe and understand Christ's
Spirit. Our mission of being disciples and making disciples cannot be done in our own human strength. We need the strength of
Christ's own Spirit alive in us to help us be disciples and to
empower us to help others become disciples too.

In other words, apart from the Spirit of Christ, we can do nothing. But with Christ's Spirit filling us, we can do anything God
wants us to do.

One of the names for the Spirit of Christ is *Holy Spirit,* which
means that when God's Spirit enters our lives, we are filled with
an urge towards being holy, pure, clean, good, and godly.

We all know there are plenty of other urges in humans—urges
toward lust, greed, anger, laziness, and pride. Growing as disciples

means learning to surrender to the Holy Spirit, not to those other darker urges.

The Holy Spirit is also called "the Spirit of God." This brings us to the edge of a great mystery, which theologians call the Trinity—that the one true and living God exists as a community of Father, Son, and Holy Spirit. This mystery is not an explanation of God; rather, it is an admission that God's being lies beyond our full comprehension. It means that in the one true and living God, there is love, communication, fellowship, and dynamic unity. It also means that God is best known not through abstract reasoning or coercive dogmatism, but through the unfolding of the story of God's self-revelation, first through the story of God as Creator and Father as embodied in the Jewish people, then through the stories of Jesus the Son, which we have in the Gospels, and then through the story of the Spirit of God active in both the church and the world, sent into us to transform us and to empower us to transform our world.

The Holy Spirit, the Spirit of Christ, the Spirit of God—this is God as we experience God in our lives today. When Jesus says, "I will be with you always," he is saying, "My Spirit is with you; my Spirit is in you."

This is encouraging to know, because often it is very hard being a disciple.

Sometimes we are very tempted to give up. But Jesus promised us that we are never alone. Being a disciple means being a person in whom Christ's Spirit is alive and active.

Are you empowered by God's Spirit?

A good analogy can be made to breathing. God's Spirit is like breath: air is all around us, but we also need air inside us. How do we get air inside us? By breathing—by opening up and taking it in. Similarly, disciples develop practices that help them keep their lives filled with the fresh wind of God's Spirit. These practices include prayer, fasting, worship, contemplation, journaling, fellowship, solitude, serving, giving, and accountability. These practices are not merely ends in themselves; they are ways for us to stay full of the Spirit of Christ, who is with us always.

Maybe you have imagined what it would be like to have lived in Jesus' day and to be one of the twelve original disciples, like Peter, James, or John. The fact is, Jesus is every bit as real and present to you as he was to them, because his Spirit—though invisible like the air we breathe or the wind that fills a sailboat's sails—is with us even now.

Say or write a prayer asking God to help you more fully experience the reality of the risen Christ, his Spirit alive within you.

Lesson 6 Review

Disciples are empowered.

Lesson 7: Disciples Live in Hope

Jesus' final words in Matthew are, "I am with you always, to the end of the age." The words, "the end of the age," are both mysterious and important.

Disciples live with a special sense of history. They believe they are part of an unfolding story, a drama, a meaningful flow of events that has come from somewhere, and is going somewhere. The story began with creation. It continued with the crisis of our disconnection from God. God responded to the crisis by calling the Jewish people to bear witness to the one true and living God. But his goal was never to keep that knowledge to an elite group alone. His goal was to bless the world through one blessed people. Jesus came to open up the door wide to the whole world, and he sent us to be his Spirit-empowered agents, being and making disciples around the world, as we have seen, "of all nations."

How will the story end?

Jesus himself painted many word pictures of the ending of the story, as did many of the prophets in Scripture. In summary, at the end, all God's purposes will be fulfilled. Good will win, and evil will be banished. God's dream for all creation will come true. This is wonderful news for those who seek God and God's justice, but it carries an ominous warning for those who are complacent, careless, or rebellious towards God.

At the end there will be a reckoning for how we lived our lives—including both answering to God for our wrongdoings, and receiving God's approval for even the smallest of kindnesses. Those who were poor, oppressed, and disadvantaged in this life will be compensated in the end, and from those to whom much was given in this life, much will be expected at the end. Jesus assures his disciples that any sacrifice they make in his cause in this life will be more than compensated "at the end of the age."

Disciples need this perspective, because Jesus promised that in this world, we will have plenty of troubles. He tells us that being his disciples will not be easy. Sometimes we will be misunderstood and sometimes even persecuted. Sometimes we will be tempted to give up, because living for greed and self can seem so much more rewarding (in the short term) than living for love and goodness. Sometimes we will become discouraged by our own failures and weaknesses. But disciples, who have confidence in Jesus, are determined to keep living for higher purposes than "normal" pursuits of money, possessions, pleasures, revenge, leisure, and security. Since we are assured of forgiveness because of God's mercy to us in Christ, we do not let our own failures defeat us. We fall down, and we get up again and keep going on our journey.

In the end, disciples believe, it will all be worthwhile.

It is impossible to be a wholehearted disciple without this eternal perspective. To be a disciple means to live with this larger sense of reality—one that spans beyond this age, this time, this life on earth.

Jesus said he would be with us until the end of the age, and we live with the confidence that he will be waiting for us beyond this life on earth. Whether we pass beyond this life through the "normal" portal of death, or through some sort of apocalyptic end to history as we know it, as disciples we live with a certain hope that gives us the freedom to take risks, to make sacrifices, and to live life with wildness, passion, and freedom for God.

Some people are prone to frantic or spectacular speculations about the end of the world or the second coming of Christ. History makes it clear, as did Jesus' plain teachings, that these speculations are unwise. It is far wiser for us as disciples to simply live with a larger span of reference than our short lives, our brief history, our limited vision.

If someone were to evaluate your life as an impartial observer, would he say your life makes sense in terms of this present age, or would he say your life is being lived with a larger span of reference that includes a life beyond this one?

Do you have confidence that there is a life beyond this life? Is your confidence sufficient to free you to take risks, make sacrifices, and live life with a wildness and freedom for God? Do you live in hope—believing that in the end, God's dream for all of creation will come true?

Lesson 7 Review

Let's review these seven lessons of discipleship rooted in the last words of Matthew's Gospel.

Disciples have confidence in the full authority of Jesus.
Disciples are people with a mission.
Disciples are identified as disciples.
Disciples teach.
Disciples have a global/local vision.
Disciples are empowered.
Disciples live in hope.

If we engage in spiritual friendship with others, if we try to help others become disciples, we will find our own understanding of what it means to be a Christian changing. We will find our purpose aligning around being and making disciples of Jesus Christ in authentic community for the good of the world. We will see our lives as a dance to God's beautiful song, and we will feel it our incomparable honor through spiritual friendship to help others feel the song's wonder and be swept up into its graceful beauty and resounding joy.

Appendix 2:

Suggestions for Group or Individual Study

Bible Studies

Here are some passages that recount some of Jesus' conversations with spiritual friends he encountered in his journeys. Read these passages and ask what you can learn from each individually, and then from the stories taken together, about spiritual friendship Jesus-style.

Matthew 19:16 ff
John 4:4 ff
Matthew 15:21 ff
Luke 5:12 ff
John 3:1 ff
John 8:1 ff
Luke 19:1 ff

Here are some passages that reflect Jesus' general feelings towards people.

Matthew 9:36–38
    (contrast with John 7:47–49)
Matthew 14:14, 15:32, 20:34

Here are a few passages that illustrate the first apostles' communication with unconvinced people.

Acts 17:22 ff
Acts 10:1 ff

Here are some passages from the New Testament that talk about our interaction with people who do not share our faith and commitment.

Colossians 4:4 ff
1 Peter 3:15–17
Matthew 5:13–17

Here are some passages from the Old Testament that reaffirm the understanding that we people of faith are blessed to be a blessing to everyone (described in these passages as "the nations" or "the peoples").

Genesis 12:1–3
Psalm 67
Isaiah 42:6–7; 49:6

My Favorite Books on Evangelism

Walker Percy, *The Message in the Bottle* (Picador USA, 2000): The title essay is worth the price of the book, and along with "Notes for a Novel about the End of the World," offers some of the best insights into evangelism anywhere.

Mark Mittelberg, Bill Hybels, *Becoming a Contagious Christian* (Zondervan, 1996), and *Building a Contagious Church* (Zondervan, 2000): Mittelberg and Hybels, writing more from a modern (rather than postmodern) perspective, offer wonderful help to potential spiritual friends by showing that all evangelism isn't buttonholing people on the street.

Rick Warren, *The Purpose-Driven Church* (Zondervan, 1995). I first heard Rick share this material in 1985, when I was a college English professor. As I heard Rick share the story of Saddleback Valley Community Church, for the first time in my life I could envision a church that had authentic evangelism running through its veins, and for the first time I sensed that God might be inviting me to leave teaching to do this kind of church-based disciple-making. I literally would not be doing what I am doing if not for Rick's impact on my life.

George Hunter, *The Celtic Way of Evangelism* (Abingdon, 2000), and *How to Reach Secular People* (Abingdon, 1992): George Hunter was one of the first writers I found who was sensitive to the changes taking place in evangelism as we move beyond modernity, and he does a good job of describing some of the trends.

Rick Richardson, *Evangelism Outside the Box* (IVP, 2000) and Tom Clegg and Warren Bird, *Lost in America* (Group, 2001): These are two of the first books that challenge Christians to understand how the modern-postmodern shift impacts the ways we engage in disciple-making. They are full of fresh insight and practical encouragement.

Robert Webber, *Journey to Jesus* (Abingdon, 2001). What Robert Webber has previously done for worship in *Ancient-Future Faith*—namely, bringing ancient resources to the aid of the contemporary church—he does for evangelism and discipleship in this new book, which contains rich insight about the conversion process and the value of rite-of-passage events.

My Favorite Movies Related to Evangelism/ Disciple-Making

These movies are great for a group discussion.

The Big Kahuna: Brace yourself for some tough language, and for some even tougher insights into what evangelism/spiritual friendship is and isn't about in this hard-hitting and off-beat film starring Danny Devito and Kevin Spacey.

The Mission: A musical and visual feast, this film depicts a holistic process of disciple-making playing out in the real world of history, agony, brokenness, and beauty.

Steel Magnolias: A Southern lady loses her daughter, and a *religious* friend shows how not to be a *spiritual* friend.

Contact, The Truman Show, and *Mindwalk:* If you are trying to get a feel for the differences between the modern and postmodern worlds, these two films are hard to beat, and offer fertile ground for lengthy conversations.

My Favorite Books to Give to a Spiritually Seeking Friend

Mere Christianity (C. S. Lewis, Harper San Francisco, 2001): The twentieth century's greatest apologist's second-greatest apologetic work (after *The Chronicles of Narnia,* which are also hereby included in my list).

The Case for Christ (Zondervan, 1998); *The Case for Faith* (Zondervan, 2000): Lee Strobel writes state-of-the-art apologetics within a modern (rather than postmodern) context, and he does so winsomely, intelligently, and clearly. This book has helped, and will help, many, many people.

Letters from a Skeptic (Chariot Victor, 1994): Greg Boyd and his father, Edward, share a cordial, honest, and thoughtful dialogue about faith and doubt.

Finding Faith (Brian McLaren, Zondervan, 1999): Pardon the self-promotion, but *Finding Faith* is still the only book I am aware of that attempts a more postmodern (rather than strictly modern) apologetic. It is important to take seriously the suggestion in the introduction to read the book in whatever order one desires; reading from the first to last page straight through would not be best for many readers.

Traveling Mercies (Anne Lamott, Anchor, 2000): If you never thought a book on the spiritual journey could make you laugh—and could include a supply of four-letter words— you shouldn't miss this treasure, which is worth giving to a lot of friends.

Finding Faith

A Self-Discovery Guide for Your Spiritual Quest

Brian D. McLaren

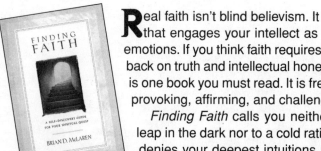

Real faith isn't blind believism. It is a process that engages your intellect as well as your emotions. If you think faith requires turning your back on truth and intellectual honesty, then this is one book you must read. It is fresh, thought-provoking, affirming, and challenging.

Finding Faith calls you neither to a blind leap in the dark nor to a cold rationalism that denies your deepest intuitions and spiritual longings. Rather, in the tradition of C. S. Lewis's *Mere Christianity* and M. Scott Peck's *The Road Less Traveled,* it summons you to reflection and honesty. With logic, passion, and an evenhandedness that the thinking person will appreciate, this book helps you face your obstacles to faith by focusing not on what to believe but on how to believe.

Whether you want to strengthen the faith you have, renew the faith you lost, or discover faith for the first time, *Finding Faith* can coach, inspire, encourage, and guide you. And it can help you discover, through a dynamic, authentic, and growing faith, more in life than you'd ever imagined or hoped for.

Hardcover   ISBN: 0-310-22542-6
Softcover   ISBN: 0-310-23838-2
www.crcc.org
www.emergentvillage.org

Pick up a copy today at your favorite bookstore!

GRAND RAPIDS, MICHIGAN 49530

w w w . z o n d e r v a n . c o m

Carpe Mañana

Leonard Sweet

**The Message Never Changes.
But Our Methods Must.**

If God so loved the world . . . then we ought to, too. But how? While the church dreams of old wineskins, the future is arriving, and the world around us has undergone a radical transformation. Those of us over thirty are no longer natives of a modern culture, but immigrants in a postmodern society that speaks the language of cyberspace, grapples with the implications of robotics, nanotechnology, and bioengineering, and looks everywhere but to the church for spiritual and moral guidance.

But the gospel sun, far from setting, is poised to shine on this new frontier—provided we'll seize tomorrow and its unprecedented opportunities. The possibilities are limitless for those of us who choose to live as Jesus lived, as people of our time and culture. *Carpe Mañana* helps us go native. In nine "naturalization classes," Leonard Sweet speeds us toward influence in this postmodern world—a world hungry to encounter the God who knows its soul, speaks its language, and loves it with an all-transforming love.

Also available in condensed e-book edition, The Dawn Mistaken for Dusk.

Seize this resource at your favorite bookstore or ebook provider!

Hardcover   ISBN: 0-310-23947-8   ebook   ISBN: 0-310-23223-6
Softcover   ISBN: 0-310-25012-9

A Is for Abductive

The Language of the Emerging Church

**Leonard Sweet, Brian D. McLaren,
and Jerry Haselmayer**

An essential guide for understanding the language and ideas of the 21st century

This witty but substantive primer explores the basic concepts and vernacular of postmodern ministry. This "postmodern ministry-for-dummies" will help "immigrants" learn to speak PSL (postmodern as a second language), so they can better live, minister, and make a difference in the emerging postmodern context.

Topics covered include:

- Abductive Method/Augmentation
- Branding/Blur/Body/Be-live
- Outside the Box Thinking/Open-endedness/Outward-focused/Organic
- PALS (Partnership/Alliance/Liaisons/Strategic Collaborations)/Paradox

Softcover ISBN: 0-310-24356-4

SoulSalsa

17 Surprising Steps for
Godly Living in the 21st Century

Leonard Sweet

Wake up and dance!

Leonard Sweet wants to show you the ins and outs of living an old-fashioned faith in the newfangled times. In his engaging, wonderful, thought-bytes style, Sweet invites you to

Mezuzah your universe • Do dirt and do the dishes • Cycle to Church
Give history a shove • Cheer rivals from the bench • Dance the salsa

SoulSalsa unpacks it all in ways that can change how you live if you let them. You can be a man or woman who walks the ancient path of a disciple in the world of the future. Because the future is now—and now is the time to practice the "17 Lifestyle Requirements for Membership in the Postmodern Body of Christ." Time to enter the dance of a culture that desperately needs to see your moves.

Check out the *SoulSalsa* song, playing on a Christian music station near you—or download the mp3 from *www.SoulSalsa.com.*

Softcover   ISBN: 0-310-24280-0
Abridged Audio Pages® Cassettes   ISBN: 0-310-23482-4

www.Soulsalsa.com
www.pm4j.com

SoulTsunami

Sink or Swim in
New Millennium Culture

Leonard Sweet

The best way to wake up to the dawn: Take a swim!

Before you go out and seize the new day for Christ, you'll need a little morning exercise. Jump into *SoulTsunami!* Sure, the water's cold and rough, but you'll know which way to swim if you grab the ten Life Rings Sweet provides to keep your head above water.

The Life Rings explore critical factors that define postmodern culture—from its spiritual longings, to its relationship with technology, to its global renaissance in art and invention, and more. With each come intellectual and spiritual exercises to prepare pastors, lay leaders, and other influential Christians for effective interaction with the new millennium world.

As your passionate and prophetic swimming coach, Sweet will make you remove your tunnel-vision goggles and feel the sting of the swelling postmodern flood. He will encourage and affirm you and the rest of God's lifeguard team—the church—helping you build the stamina required to rescue a world out to sea.

Softcover   ISBN: 0-310-24312-2
Abridged Audio Pages® Cassettes   ISBN: 0-310-22712-7

www.SoulTsunami.com
www.pm4j.com